My Life on a Frozen Lake

My Life on a Frozen Lake

GUIDE TO THE TWELVE STEPS OF RECOVERY

Howard P.

Table of Contents

Dedication

THIS BOOK IS DEDICATED TO *my wife Pat, without whose love and support it would have never happened; and to our children Timothy, Michael, and Annie, who without Pat's love and support would have never happened.*

To Frank Giroux, who was my greatest teacher.

To all of my sponsors in the Program: Kenny S., George C., John H., Charles C., and Bob B., without whose love, patience, wisdom, and time I would have missed most of what I have been and am being given.

To all my sponsees throughout the years whom I love and to whom I am grateful.

And finally, to everyone who finds value in this book in their struggles to recover from their seemingly hopeless states of mind and body.

In Love and Service
Howard P.

Foreward

THESE STORIES AND THIS GUIDE to the Twelve Steps of Recovery were not intended to become a published book. How that came about is briefly described in the Preface that follows. The writer has serious misgivings about having it published, most of which are related to his ego and fear of criticism from other members of the program. However, others have offered to pay for publishing this book in an effort to make it available to anyone who thinks they might benefit from it. Neither the individuals paying for the publication nor the writer are going to profit monetarily from publishing this guide. The cost for the book will be equal to the publisher's cost for printing and distributing it.

Preface

§

On August 4, 1985, I celebrated my 13th AA birthday. We had just moved to Chandler, Arizona from Culver City, California, where my wife, Pat, and I had raised our three children, Tim, Mike, and Anne. I was a Technical Section Manager in the Systems Engineering Department at Hughes Helicopters Company, which had moved us to Arizona. At the AA Meeting that night someone asked me "How did you get sober in August when it is so hot?" I immediately knew the answer. "Because that was as quick as I could make it after New Year's Eve."

Those 13 years had been the best 13 years I had had in my life. In addition to moving to Arizona where I had job security and a much lower cost of living, many things were happening for Pat and I in Alanon and AA that promised an accelerated growth of goodness in our lives.

I had joined AA in July, 1972, and I had met the most helpful people I could have met. Kenny S. was my first sponsor and was the perfect guy to help me get started. Kenny's sponsor Frank G. was the first guy Kenny introduced me to and he turned out to be the best mentor in the Program that I could have possibly had. Westside AA Meetings also fit me like a glove.

My first Home Group, the Culver City Studio Group, was the oldest meeting on the Westside and had two meetings a week: a Beginner's Meeting and a Speaker's Meeting.

The Westside old-timers focused on the Big Book and the 12 Steps; and there were many Step Study Meetings that followed "*The Twelve Steps and Twelve Tradition.*" But Southern California AA was the "hotbed" of AA speaker meetings. We had some of the icons of AA Speakers sharing every week at meetings on the Westside: Chuck C., Jack B., Norm A., Alabam C., Flo D., Don G., Johnny A., Tommy W., "Ski" A., Cliff R., Clint H., Johnny H., Clancy I., to name a few. As my AA life evolved I had three different sponsors during that first 13 years: Kenny S., George C. and John H.. Kenny, along with his sponsor Frank, got me started in Meetings, Service work, and in my sober marriage. George C. went through the Steps with me two times and John H. had guided me through them 3 times during that first 13 years. Also, I had slowly become a fairly frequent Speaker at AA Conferences throughout the country. During those years in California I had also became the sponsor for a growing group of AA members and that group of guys got larger after we moved to Arizona.

We had not lived in Arizona long and I decided that while the AA in Arizona was more austere than it was in Southern California, in many ways it was more fundamental. I also discovered that the "icons' I had listened to and became friends with in California were hardly known in Arizona. Inasmuch as I was sponsoring guys in both States I thought it might be helpful to prepare a "Guide to the Twelve Steps" which I hoped would include the best things I had learned from both places. Then, right after my 13th AA Birthday I read in the book "*Pass*

It On: The Story of Bill Wilson and How the AA Message Reached the World" (pages 351 through 354) that Bill W. had written the essays on the Steps for the 12 and 12, not to change them as they are described in the Big Book, but to "deepen and broaden" the experience of the Steps for the old-timer and newcomer alike. I understood this to mean that Bill was suggesting that we work each Step first from the Big Book, and then that Step from the 12 and 12, maintaining that sequence through all Twelve Steps. I started through the Steps again, following that guidance, and it was the most life changing experience I have had with the Steps. Part of that experience was that "coincidentally" I was gradually opening up to the understanding that the Spirit of God is now and always had been active in my life.

My sponsor John H., passed on after we had lived in Arizona for a while, and Charles C. became my sponsor. When Charles joined John and so many others in the AA Meetings in the other room, I asked Bob B., of St. Paul, Minnesota to be my sponsor. I suppose this is true for most of us but each sponsor has been the perfect guy for that time. Every one of them has given me a wonderful growing experience and in each instance my life has continued to get better in the face of growing obstacles, many associated with getting older in life.

Later in the book I share my meditation experience about a frozen lake in a broader and deeper context. But here I want to address the metaphorical meaning intended by the title. When I was 13 years sober I was given an assignment at work which I didn't believe I could do satisfactorily and that such a failure would destroy my career. I was filled with dread when my boss insisted that I was going to have to take this assignment.

The next morning, my meditation started by my focusing on this dreadful assignment, but I was soon able to focus on my current meditation practice and when my timer went off to end the meditation I experienced a sense of ease and comfort. I knew that I did not want to back out of the meditation right then or I would be backing into the dread.

I remember asking: "Why? Why do I have to meditate to have a sense of ease and comfort?" Then, as if in answer to my question I saw in my mind's eye a frozen lake. And, because it was my vision (or my fantasy) I knew that the ice was as thick as the laws of physics would let the ice get. I also knew that that ice would support the weight of a Sherman Tank.

After a few seconds pause, the thought came to me as if it was from a spoken voice: "That is right Howard. And walking across the ice on the frozen lake is a good metaphor for living your life a day at a time; be Careful because it is slippery. And if you are not convinced that the ice is thick enough to support you, you will dread every step you take. And in the same way, if you do not believe your life is supported you will experience dread in every day of your life."

I spent a few minutes contemplating that experience and then I backed out of the meditation believing that I had just been told by a Powerful Being that **IT** had my back in whatever I was doing. This was the essential beginning of a greater goodness that could have only happened in that mystical way. Although it has taken years to get here I now experience a personally satisfactory conscious partnership with the Spirit of the Universe underlying the totality of things and guiding me in this entire business of living.

If we are not convinced that we are being supported in our life we see fear as "an evil and corroding thread" drawn through "the fabric of our existence." Our self reliance ultimately fails us. "Self reliance is good as far as it goes, but it doesn't go far enough." If, on the other hand, we are convinced that we are supported we are living on a different basis: "the basis of trusting and relying upon God. "

Working the Twelve Steps of recovery as a way of life brings about a gradual transition from having "an evil and corroding thread" of fear drawn "through the fabric of our existence" to a spiritual consciousness of God pulling a golden thread through every circumstance and event in our life.

From time to time I would update the "Guide to the 12 Steps" with my changing view and experience of the Steps. A little over a year ago, I was meeting with a guy named Mike S., who I had been sponsoring for a while, and he told me something to the effect that, "I read your newest version of that Guide to the Steps and you really have a lot of good stuff in there."

I laughed and said, "I think I do too Mike, but I have to rewrite it some way to make it interesting for the people I sponsor. I can't seem to get them to read it the way it is written."

"Well, I read it." Mike responded.

"I know, Mike," I answered, "but I suspect that you read the first 10 or 15 pages and then you skimmed the rest. Evelyn Woods would be proud of the way you guys read through that Step Guide."

I not only thought that was the truth, but I also thought it was funny. For the younger people, Evelyn Woods invented speed reading back in the 1950's and 60's. I think God can see her influence in our prayers also.

Several weeks later Mike called me. He followed our exchange of greetings by telling me, "I have carefully read your Step Guide now and I want to share some thoughts with you. What I found there was that you have been given a wonderful life because of the spiritual practices you have developed in your life from working the Steps. Some of this stuff I had never heard before and I am sure I want to try it. I could also see that you have worked very hard to document your experiences in the Steps and to pass that along to your sponsee's. I know that this is what we are expected to do when we have good Programs. So, as my contribution, I would like to make this guide available to a larger audience than your sponsees. With your permission I would like to help publish it with you and make it available to everyone who might want it."

I responded to Mike's offer by explaining that when I sent the guide to my sponsor Bob B he had quickly told me he didn't think I should write a book. Soon after Mike and my phone conversation, I got a call from Bob and he told me that he had read the guide more carefully and while he would probably come to his senses later, he thought it did contain some insights about the steps that might justify publishing it as a book. These "coincidental" phone calls resulted in me discussing that possibility with some of the other people who had used the guide to work the steps. I received much more encouragement than discouragement from that group of guys.

I then circulated a series of rewrites of the guide through a growing group of people. Mike and Joan S invited me to go over the guide with a group of Joan's sponsees at their home and the comments I got back particularly from Mike and Joan, resulted in extensive rewrites to include more stories of my personal experiences. I also sent a number of drafts to friends in the program which resulted in the decision to put most of the science in Appendix I, "Science tells us so, we have no reason to doubt it" in the back of the book.

The process was exciting and discouraging and many individuals I talk with frequently not only provided great suggestions for improvement but encouragement to continue on. I want to acknowledge that the best parts of this book are the results of those suggestions and encouragement. The weaknesses are all mine. I want to acknowledge the valuable contributions of Bob B of St. Paul MN; Charlie P of Austin TX; Steve P of CA; Dr. Mike W, Mike and Joan S, Tracy N, Tom L, Mike F, all from the Phoenix AZ area; and all the others who know who they are. I thank you for your faith and dedication.

Introduction

§

THOSE OF YOU WHO HAVE heard me share at an AA meeting have probably heard the "Baby Elephant" story. One exception would be when Clancy arranged for me to be invited to give a 37 minute talk at his home group and I deleted that story from my 45 minute 'canned' talk only to learn that telling that story was a prime reason I had been invited to speak in the first place. I have not left it out since, even if I am talking on the history of the Washingtonians.

Anyway, the story is when I was a kid in a small Kansas farm community in the late 1930's I watched a travelogue movie about training elephants in India. They started the training of the baby elephants by tying a rope tightly to their right front leg with the other end of the rope tied to a tree. In this way the baby elephant is taught that when the rope is tight it is futile to keep pulling against it. Throughout the elephant's life the trainer reinforces this lesson. At the end of the movie they show a huge elephant, strong enough to drag a tree trunk out of the forest, being held by a rope tied to a stake that had been driven into the ground. The big elephant was free to walk around in the area, but when the staked rope got tight on his leg he stopped pulling. The rope didn't hold the elephant; the stake didn't hold the elephant; what held the elephant was the limiting belief that the trainer had imposed on him when he was a baby.

When I was growing up in this Kansas farm community I was taught thousands of baby elephant beliefs just like that. Gradually, over my lifetime, many of those beliefs had to be unlearned before I could experience a sense of well-being. For example, in Sunday school I was taught that I was separate from God; that God was up in Heaven while I was stuck in this little town in Kansas. I was taught that God would withhold goodness from me if I didn't behave the way He wanted me to behave and that I was going to go to Hell forever if I didn't believe and do as He wanted. I was taught that God could and would intervene with natural law to my benefit if I otherwise pleased him and if I prayed hard enough. In my community I was taught that I must become an individual achiever and that I must win the competition in order to become the best and thereby experience a feeling of well-being. My dad, an alcoholic, beat me physically and emotionally so that in the long run the best feeling I can remember having before finding sobriety in AA was a state of low grade alert. In the book Alcoholics Anonymous that is described as feelings of impending calamity.

I was five or six years old the first time I remember praying and knowing who I was praying to and what I was praying for. It was Sunday morning and our Protestant Preacher led us in a fervent prayer to beseech God to not let it rain until after wheat harvest. Much to my dismay it rained that day and night; it hailed; and the wind blew. The storm destroyed the entire wheat crop in Sumner County Kansas. While no one got after me about it I knew that it was my fault that it rained. I knew that I had not been behaving the way God wanted me to and I believed everyone else was behaving. Now, if when you are five or six years old you assume the entire responsibility for destroying the Kansas wheat crop, what you are experiencing is an Ego Problem. My ego, basing my sense of well-being on my controlling things that I lack the power to control was then, and is now, the root of my problem.

When I was 12 or 13 years old I drank my first half of a half pint of whiskey and I experienced a sense of well-being for the first time in my life. I remember saying to myself, "This is what it is like to feel good. This is what they mean when they say "Let's go have a few drinks and get to feeling good." That quickly became the obsessive baby elephant belief that almost destroyed my life.

The progression of my obsession to drink was similar to most of the stories you hear in AA meetings: Initially I drank to feel good; then I drank to be somebody special. Later, as a young husband, father and entry level Engineer I drank to relieve immobilizing anxiety so I could do process analysis work and write technical reports. This led to a series of promotions: from the initial entry level to an Engineer; to a Senior Engineer; and, then to an Engineering Manager. Promotions which I believe I would not have gotten if I hadn't drank. Not surprisingly, continuing to drink alcohol led to my demotion and then to Alcoholics Anonymous.

In Psychology 101 we were taught that when we learn something new (a baby elephant belief), it is stored in our brain's memory bank where a "force field" is set up to screen out and reject any new information that conflicts with that initial belief. Our efforts to retain the conflicting information causes us to experience an uneasiness and discomfort called cognitive dissonance. Hence, we sometimes stay locked into baby elephant beliefs much longer than they are useful, if they were ever useful. The strength in this process lies in only having to learn to walk, talk, run, and myriad other behaviors one time. A problem with this process is that needed newer information which appears to conflict with the initial belief results in cognitive dissonance which adds to our difficulty in learning the new stuff.

In my early Engineering career I encountered this problem when I had to learn the binary numbering system which at first appeared to conflict with the decimal numbering system that I had learned as a "baby elephant." Sometime later my daughter Anne, who was taught the "new math" in elementary school, bought me a Tee Shirt that read: "THERE ARE ONLY 10 KINDS OF PEOPLE, THOSE WHO UNDERSTAND BINARY NUMBERS AND THOSE THAT DON'T."

I encountered this problem big time when I came to AA, and I am still encountering it. Bill W.'s admonition: "Some of us have tried to hold on to our old ideas and the result was nil until we let go absolutely. . ." does not only apply to newcomers. Father Richard Rohr points out in his book "*The Immortal Diamond: The Search For Our True Self*" that "Spirituality tends to be more about unlearning than learning. And when the slag and dross are removed, that which evokes reverence is right there waiting."

In preparing this Guide to the Twelve Steps of Recovery I have been very conscious of Dr. Bob's 'last talk' to the AA Fellowship where he saw fit to lay a little emphasis on the simplicity of our program. "Let's not louse it all up with Freudian complexes and things that are interesting to the scientific mind but have very little to do with our actual AA work."

In regard to ". . . things that are interesting to the scientific mind only . . ." I have simply tried to widen and deepen Bill's spiritual comments in the Big Book, that "Science tells us so. We have no reason to doubt it."

Insofar as Freudian complexes are concerned, I have also kept in mind Sigmund Freud's letter to Wilhelm Fliess, dated 22 December 1897, as quoted by Michael Fitzpatrick on page 106 in his book *Dr. Bob & Bill W. Speak*, "The insight has dawned on me that masturbation is the one major habit, the 'primary addiction,' and it is only as a substitute and replacement for it that the other addictions—alcohol, morphine, tobacco, and the like—come into existence." I have also read in an article I found on the internet that Dr. Freud recommended the use of cocaine in the treatment of alcoholism. I have no idea how to work that stuff into a Guide to the Twelve Steps of Recovery without lousing up their simplicity.

I agree with Dr. Bob that we should keep it simple, but I don't believe his last talk was intended to convey that we should dumb the program down. As Bill W. notes on page 93 of the Big Book, the new man "...can choose any conception (of God) he likes, provided it makes sense to him."

Several Doctor's Opinions

§

WHEN I WAS A KID in the fifth grade we had to read a book and give an oral report on the book to the class. When Mary was called on to tell us about her book, she stood before the class and reported: "My book was about penguins. It told me more about penguins than I wanted to know." And she returned to her seat. This part of the Guide may tell you more about alcoholic brain chemistry than you want to know.

I want to emphasize at the start that I know very little about neurology, brain chemistry, neural plasticity or Science. In this guide I have shared instances in my experience with the Steps which seemed to me to directly relate to what is described in the technical literature I have researched on the brain chemistry of an alcoholic/drug addict.

Bill W. has written in the Doctor's Opinion, page xxiv, Second Edition, of the Big Book: "In this statement he (Dr. Silkworth) confirms what we who have suffered alcoholic torture must believe---that the body of the alcoholic is quite as abnormal as his mind." Then on page 7, Bill writes, "Best of all, I met a kind doctor who explained that though certainly selfish and foolish, I had been seriously ill, bodily and mentally. . . . The curve of my declining moral and bodily health fell off like a ski-jump." . . . "We are equally positive that once he takes any alcohol whatever into his system, something happens, both in the bodily and mental sense, which makes it virtually impossible for him to stop." (Page 22) "No person likes to think he is bodily and mentally different from his fellows." (Page 30) Dr. Silkworth's insistence that alcoholics are bodily and mentally different from their fellows, and sets them "apart as a distinct entity," actually became bedrock on which later research could be built. In *"AA Comes of Age"* Bill tells us that Dr. Silkworth gave us the words that would deflate the toughest alcoholic ego. These essential passwords: *"**An obsession of the mind** coupled **with an allergy of the body**"* have led every alcoholic that is sober today through the A.A. program into surrender and sobriety.

Dr. Silkworth's indispensable description helped guide every sober alcoholic to begin to understand their hopeless and helpless condition. These were contributions which certainly served to qualify Dr. Silkworth as "very much a founder of A.A." Over recent years, several Doctors of various scientific specialties have discovered a growing body of scientific evidence exposing the brain chemistry and functions from which the "obsessions of the mind" and "the phenomenon of craving" are created and nurtured. This new information can provide a deeper understanding of the nature of our alcoholic condition and, more importantly, a deeper understanding of how working the Twelve Steps of recovery affectively address these conditions. As Bill predicted, "God will constantly disclose more to you and to us." (Page 164)

When I first came into the program, one of the "old-timers" in my home group, had explained some of this stuff to me, and he gave me a copy of the October, 1968 *"Grapevine"* which included an article by Stanley E. Gitlow, MD, Associate Clinical Professor of Medicine, Mt. Sinai Medical School, New York, N. Y., titled *"A Pharmacological Approach to Alcoholism."* Dr. Gitlow was one of the leading spokesmen for the AMA on the disease aspects of Alcoholism and Drug Addiction during the 1960's and 1970's.

This article is a lecture Dr. Gitlow gave to a group of medical students at Mount Sinai Medical School that describes the functioning of the brain as a complex series of circuits which transmit impulses from one point to another within the brain and throughout the human body. Dr. Gitlow explains that this functioning depends on a group of biochemical events with which alcohol and other drugs interfere with in order to provide short term relief from anxiety; and emphasizes that this short term relief is always followed by more anxiety than was initially experienced. He describes this process from its beginnings as a simple hang-over to Delirium Tremors and death. He argues that there are no sedative drugs that offer temporary relief from anxiety that do not increase the anxiety following the brief period of relief. ***The fiddler must always be paid.***

Dr. Gitlow notes that a characteristic feature of alcoholism is that the individual goes back and does it again and again, even though he loses his job, health and family. *The definition of the disease includes not just addiction, but also compulsivity.* What is it about this class of people that in spite of these losses they are compelled to repeat taking the first drink time and time again?

Dr. Gitlow suggests that these individuals initially have a higher level of anxiety on a biochemical basis than normal drinkers. What is normal for them is higher than what is normal for the average temperate drinker because of a biochemical imbalance within the brain. They do not feel like other people until their anxiety level is artificially (and temporarily) brought down by sedatives (a family of drugs which includes alcohol). This is repeated over and over, starting with higher than normal tension, drinking, short-term pleasure, followed by long term pain; then experiencing still higher tension, drinking again, with a resulting longer term pain; a cycle that can be endured by the individual over an extensive period of time. In the long run, however, a point is reached when decreasing the anxiety to a really lower state is difficult, no matter how much alcohol is taken. This is because the agitating effects from all the drinks are additive. All of our stories clearly describe this progressive experience of getting worse, never better, over the period of our drinking.

More recently a book entitled, *"The Selfish Brain: Learning From Addiction,"* written by Robert L. DuPont, M.D., first published by the American Psychiatric Press, Inc., in 1997 (most recently published by Hazelden) that presents a more detailed description on how brain cells pass information through releasing chemicals into the connecting synapses. These chemicals are known as neural transmitters and include Norepinephrine, messenger for anger and fear in the fight-or-flight center; Dopamine and Serotonin, messengers for the pleasure center; and Endorphins, characterized by Dr. DuPont as "Nature's Heroin."

A still more recent book published in 2011, and written by Louis Teresi, MD, in collaboration with Harry Haroutunian, MD, titled *"Hijacking the Brain: How Drugs and Alcohol Addiction Hijacks Our Brains—The Science Behind Twelve Step Recovery,"* includes a wealth of detailed data describing the alcoholic and drug addicts brain anatomy and bio-chemistry. The book cites functional magnetic resonance imaging (fMRI), positron emission tomography (PET), and single photon emission computed tomography (SPECT) and related studies showing the varying intensities of activity in different centers of the brain during different stages of alcoholism and drug addiction, as well as during recovery.

Doctors Silkworth, DuPont and Teresi each present convincing arguments that the alcoholic and the drug addict are restless, irritable and discontented; and, that they basically use alcohol and drugs to reduce pain and elevate feelings of pleasure. Dr. Teresi in particular presents evidence in brain scans of more intense activity in the 'fight or flight' center of the alcoholic's brain and less activity in the "pleasure" center when they are drinking, withdrawing or early sobriety. And both Dr. DuPont and Dr. Teresi have dedicated complete chapters of their books on Twelve Step Programs and their effectiveness in promoting recovery from alcoholism and drug addiction. Both refer to these programs as modern miracles

While these recent reports show that alcoholic's and addict's brain chemistry is unbalanced at the end of their drinking and using. They do not now provide specific data to support Dr. Gitlow's theory that the initial stress level of the alcoholic is higher and the pleasure center is lower than normal people's before they take their first drink. The scope and complexity of a study designed to prove that would be enormous. Nevertheless, it seems to me that it would be appropriate to repeat what Bill W. includes in the Big Book when he addresses Doctor Silkworth's positions that the body of the alcoholic is as abnormal as his mind. "As laymen, our opinion as to its soundness may, of course, mean little. But as ex-problem drinkers, we can say that his explanation makes good sense. It explains many things for which we cannot otherwise account."

We often hear alcoholics share that when they had their first drink ". . . it was the first time I knew what it was like to feel normal;" or, "It was the first time I had ever felt good." These, or comments like them, are met with nodding heads of approval and identification in AA meetings. How else can we explain that these alcoholic individuals "feel good for the first time" when they have their first drink, except that they have generally been biochemically spring loaded to fight or flight and their pleasure centers have remained inactive in response to normal successful experiences.

One popular medical doctor who is a member of the Program, and who heads an alcoholism and drug addiction treatment center for medical professionals, recently described the alcoholic's brain chemistry as being what I characterize as "spring loaded" to feelings of "restlessness, irritability and discontentment;" and their "pleasure centers" as being a "quart low." When I asked this doctor if research had been completed that supported Dr. Gitlow's hypothesis, he responded, "Research is currently in process, the initial results are promising; and, nothing has been published."

In the mid 1950's when I had Psychology 101, I was taught that it was impossible for the central nervous system to develop additional neurons after birth; and, that the brains functions were basically static throughout adulthood. In 2007, Dr. Norman Doidge wrote a book entitled *"The Brain That Changes Itself: Stories of Personal Triumph from the Frontiers of Brain Science,"* which is described by the New York Times as straddling the gap between science and self-help. This book is an introduction to Neuroplasticity and the scientists who are discovering and developing this science. **Neuro** is for "neuron," the nerve cells in our brains and nervous systems. **Plastic** is for "changeable, malleable, modifiable." This book includes stories about the frontiers of brain science, where scientist have shown that the brain changes its very structure with each different activity it performs, perfecting its circuits so it is better suited to the task at hand; and, that this is true of essentially all human brains.

As Dr. Gitlow explained, the brain is a switchboard having a large number of nerve cells. Actually, your brain has 100 billion nerve cells and 1000 trillion synapses (I have no idea who counted these but he had to be a very busy boy) whose function is to transmit impulses through electrical and chemical signals that create pathways through the brain cells. Dr. Doidge describes several basic principles of Neuroplasticity in his book; three of which are:

* First, "what is fired is wired." Everything we learn causes new connections to form and old connections to break based upon this principle.

- Second, "what you don't use you lose." When we stop doing something, the connections disengage. The longer we stop doing something the more disconnects take place.
- Third, when we fire a 'circuit' more frequently it takes over cells and their connections from its neighbors. In strengthening these circuits adjoining cells which are not being used otherwise are 'drafted' into the army of cells being formed for the task involved.

When we are working the steps we are literally changing our neural pathways. If you do not *use* resentment brain circuits you *lose* them. If you *fire* forgiveness circuits you wire them. Some things we repeat enough in our lives that even if we stop, the ability to restart the activity remains if we start doing it again. A common example of this is riding a bicycle; other examples for the alcoholic/drug addict would be "selfishness and self-seeking behavior" and to start drinking and using again. Keep in mind that the selfish neural transmitters are just shut off, they are not destroyed. "It is easy to let up on the spiritual program of action and rest on our laurels. We are headed for trouble if we do, for alcohol is a subtle foe." Big Book, Page 85

I want to note that the idea that the brain and its functions are not fixed throughout adulthood was also proposed by William James in 1892 in his book, *Psychology*. In fact, to me, his chapter entitled "Habit," reads very much like Dr. Doidge's descriptions of neuroplasticity. Although his book was widely read and he was widely respected as a psychologist, his ideas on 'neuroplasticity' were largely ignored.

Let's stop here for a moment and think about these facts. The fact that we are spring loaded to fight and flight to have our way coupled with our pleasure center not paying off as promised by our culture gradually resulting in acute anger/fear transforming into chronic anger (resentments) and anxiety. This process is exacerbated by the addition of alcohol and drugs to the process. The Twelve Steps of Recovery directly address this brain chemistry and structure in exactly the right sequence and increments to effectively transform our brain chemistry and circuits from fight or flight to happiness and satisfaction; from self-centeredness to God-centeredness. In light of the fact that the 12 Steps came into being and were being practiced in our program before this information on brain chemistry became available to Science validates Drs. DuPont and Teresi's description of the Twelve Steps as "Modern Miracles."

Last, but far from least, is Dr. Jill Taylor's book *"My Stroke of Insight: A Brain Scientist's Personal Journey."* Dr. Taylor's little book is about her experience with a stroke. She had gotten her PhD in Neural Anatomy and was teaching that subject at Harvard Medical School. She was a left brain person, analytical and hardworking individual achiever. She was particularly active in building a brain bank for the study of schizophrenia. In her book she describes having a stroke that disabled much of her left brain function. When she recovered her active consciousness in her right brain, she discovered who she had always been: "A spiritual being in a human body." Over an eight year period she gradually recovered her left brain functions. But with her knowledge of brain anatomy and function, coupled with a determined mindset, she was able to control that development in a manner leaving her right brain and her 'spiritual being' in charge. In reading her story I could see that it validates the impact that working the Steps can have on our brain chemistry and neural pathways, inasmuch as she utilized many of the same spiritual practices that we find in the Steps in her controlled recovery from her brain damaging stroke.

A Couple More Opinions

In his book, "*An Open Heart: Practicing Compassion in Everyday Life*," The Dalai Lama writes, "Although we all naturally aspire to be happy and wish to overcome our misery, we continue to experience pain and suffering. Why is this? . . . In our normal way of life, we let ourselves be controlled by powerful thoughts and emotions, which in turn give rise to negative states of mind. It is by this vicious circle that we perpetuate not only our unhappiness but also that of others. We must deliberately take a stand to reverse these tendencies and replace them with new habits. . . . We must nurture new inclinations by deliberately cultivating virtuous practices."

That is exactly what we do when we practice the Twelve Steps of Recovery.

In his book, "*A Journey of Awakening: A Meditators Guidebook*," Ram Dass writes: "Your ego is a set of thoughts that define your universe. It's like a familiar room built of thoughts; you see the universe through its windows. You are secure in it, but to the extent you are afraid to venture outside, it has become a prison." . . . "There is an alternative. You needn't destroy the ego to escape its tyranny. You can keep this familiar room to use as you wish, and you can be free to come and go. First you need to know that you are infinitely more than the ego room by which you define yourself." Once you know this, you have the power to change the ego from your prison to your living room . . . through working the 12 Steps of recovery.

The Twelve Steps of Recovery

§

As many AA members already know, Bill W. was in Akron, Ohio in June of 1935 where an important business opportunity collapsed. He was disappointed and was seriously considering having a drink when he decided instead to find another alcoholic to work with. He made a series of phone calls in an effort to contact an alcoholic member of the Oxford Group, a Christian group from England, where he had first found sobriety. Through these phone calls he was able to meet with Dr. Bob S., who, from that first meeting was to become a cofounding member of AA, along with Bill W.

Because the founding members of our AA Program got their spiritual beginnings in the Oxford Group, I selected parts of the book entitled *"What is the Oxford Group?"* by the author identified as 'The Laymen with the Notebook" which was first copy written in 1938. These writings describe spiritual practices and principles upon which the Twelve Steps appear to be at least partially based. I have listed below what are known as the Four Absolutes and what the author of this little book characterized as four practical spiritual activities advocated by the Oxford Group.

"To be spiritually reborn, and to live in the state in which these four points (ABSOLUTE Honesty, Purity, Unselfishness, and Love) are the guides to our life in God, the Oxford Group advocates four practical spiritual activities:"

1. "The Sharing of our sins and temptations with another Christian life given to God, and to use Sharing as Witness to help others, still unchanged, to recognize and acknowledge their sins."
2. "Surrender of our life, past, present, and future, into God's keeping and direction."
3. "Restitution to all whom we have wronged directly or indirectly."
4. "Listening to, accepting, relying on God's Guidance and carrying it out in everything we do or say, great or small."

More detailed descriptions of these 'practical spiritual activities,' are included in this little book about the Oxford Group but I decided to omit them because they are much different from the 'practical spiritual activities,' described in the Twelve Steps of recovery as eventually written by Bill W. While I did not see myself as anti-religious when I arrived in AA, when I was sober for several years I was introduced to Henry Drummond's little book *"The Greatest Thing in the World,"* and I nearly rejected those essays because they were based on St. Paul's 1st Corinthians, 13th Chapter. I was literally frightened that I might get pulled back into "the Bible Belt Christianity" I had been raised in when I was a kid, and I rejected that idea totally.

Dr. Bob's recommendation of that book was what convinced me to read it.

In Mike Fitzpatrick's book, "*Dr. Bob & Bill W. Speak*," there is a letter from Dr. Bob to Bill W., dated February 17, 1938 (page 138) where Bob was discussing a visit he had from Frank Amos, a close friend of John D. Rockefeller, Jr., wherein Dr. Bob has written: "Of course he heard some Oxford Group chatter but we tried to impress him with the fact that as far as the alcoholic group was concerned we could not be identified with the group and explained why such a setup was impossible."

So 'Alcoholics Anonymous,' which was as yet an unnamed group of recovering alcoholics, can be regarded as having separated from the Oxford Group by early 1938, by its cofounders. In Bill's undated reply to Dr. Bob's letter, which was probably written in the late spring or early summer of 1938, Bill told Dr. Bob that "Nearly everyone agrees that we should sign the volume, Alcoholics Anonymous." (Pages 141-142) So the Program of 'Alcoholics Anonymous' was taking shape as early as 1938.

Bill W. and Dr. Bob's experiences with the Oxford Group helped them form pragmatic spiritual beliefs and practices in their lives that were essential to their sobriety. The separation of "Alcoholics Anonymous" from the Oxford Group by 1938 turned out to be significant for AA's future in that Bill's ability to emphasize on Page 93-4 of the Big Book that ". . . We represent no particular faith or denomination. We are dealing only with general principles common to most denominations. . . ." became an attraction to many future members who could accept a spiritual program but could not initially accept a religious one.

In a letter dated October 30, 1940, to a member in Richmond, Virginia, Bill explains his reasons for splitting off from the Oxford Group: "I am always glad to explain myself privately that some of the Oxford Group presentation and emphasis upon the Christian message saved my life. Yet it is equally true that other attitudes of the OG nearly got me drunk again, and we long since discovered that if we were to approach alcoholics successfully, these attitudes would have to be abandoned." Bill then lists in detail eight examples of attitudes he thought had to be changed to provide the best chance for an alcoholic to recover.

I would also add that my experience has been similar to Bill's in that I think Drummond's little book *"The Greatest Thing in the World,"* transformed my life to the better. I could not have gotten sober on the Christian teachings of the Oxford Group.

When Bill W. and other AA pioneer's completed and published the first edition of the Big Book in 1939. They revised it into the second edition in 1955. On page 287 of the first printing of the second edition we find the story about the guy who wrote: "He Sold Himself Short," in the back of the Big Book and who eventually brought the program of Alcoholics Anonymous to Chicago. On page 191-92, of the second edition he writes:

"The day before I was due to go back to Chicago, a Wednesday and Dr. Bob's afternoon off, he had me down to the office and we spent three or four hours formally going through the Six-Step program as it was at that time. The six steps were:

1. Complete deflation.
2. Dependence and guidance from a Higher Power.
3. Moral Inventory.
4. Confession.
5. Restitution.
6. Continued work with other alcoholics.

Dr. Bob led me through all of these steps. At the moral inventory, he brought up some of my bad personality traits or character defects, such as selfishness, conceit, jealousy, carelessness, intolerance, ill-temper, sarcasm and resentments. We went over these at great length and then he finally asked me if I wanted these defects of character removed. When I said yes, we both knelt at his desk and prayed, each of us asking to have these defects taken away.

This picture is still vivid. If I live to be a hundred, it will always stand out in my mind. It was very impressive and I wish that every A.A. could have the benefit of this type of sponsorship today. Dr. Bob always emphasized the religious angle very strongly, then led me through the restitution step, in which I made a list of all the persons I had harmed, and worked out ways and means of slowly making restitution." Pages 191-92, Big Book

Later, in *"Alcoholics Anonymous Comes of Age,"* on page 161, Bill explains that when considering that those alcoholics, who were going to get sober in cities where AA had not yet been started, would need more detailed description of our Steps and how they work. He then describes how he sat down to expand the Steps into more than six. He was not sure how many but he relaxed and asked for guidance. He wrote for about a half hour and reached a stopping point. He counted the Steps and there were 12. He loosely connected that number with the twelve apostles. Greatly relieved he commenced to rereading what he had written.

Bill goes on to explain how "heated" discussions ensued about the language and the content of the revised version of the Six Step Program. As Joe and Charlie in their later "Big Book Comes Alive" seminars inquired: "How would you react if you came to a meeting one night and found that someone had added six more steps to the Program than it had last week?" If you have not read *"Comes of Age," and "Pass It On,"* do so as soon as possible. They are fascinating history and will enhance your appreciation of what our founders have done for us.

The Twelve Steps of Recovery as they appear in the Big Book and in the *Twelve Steps and Twelve Traditions* today:

1. We admitted we were powerless over alcohol---that our lives had become unmanageable.
2. Came to believe that a Power greater than ourselves could restore us to sanity.
3. Made a decision to turn our will and our lives over to the care of God *as we understood Him.*
4. Made a searching and fearless moral inventory of ourselves.

5. Admitted to God, to ourselves, and to another human being the exact nature of our wrongs.
6. Were entirely ready to have God remove all these defects of character.
7. Humbly asked Him to remove our shortcomings.
8. Made a list of all persons we had harmed, and became willing to make amends to them all.
9. Made direct amends to such people wherever possible, except when to do so would injure them or others.
10. Continued to take personal inventory and when we were wrong promptly admitted it.
11. Sought through prayer and meditation to improve our conscious contact with God as we understood Him, praying only for knowledge of His will for us and the power to carry that out.
12. Having had a spiritual awakening as the result of these steps, we tried to carry this message to alcoholics, and to practice these principles in all our affairs.

When I read these over a couple of times, I focus on each word and listen within myself for the deeper meaning of each word and phrase. I am aware of a simple set of life changing steps, broken down within each step in exactly the right sequence and increments which effectively address the alcoholic's unique brain chemistry and in which we can find sobriety and a spiritual way of life a day at a time for the rest of our lives.

When I was new in the program I was taught that the Program of recovery was basically described in Chapter Five, "How It Works" in the Big Book. Many of the "old-timers" looked on the 12 and 12 as a poor effort to clarify "How It Works" in the Big Book. The first time I went through the Steps I essentially relied on Chapter Five to help me work the Steps. Frank helped me with Meditation and Prayer from the 12 and 12 but most of the old-timers that claimed to have worked the 12 Steps argued that the Big Book was all we needed for that.

Later, when George C. was my sponsor and took me through the Steps a second time, he focused on Chapter Five but highlighted parts of the 12 and 12 which were very helpful. Again, this second time through the Steps transformed my life and redirected me from almost total self-centeredness to the practice of unselfish spiritual principles in my life.

My third sponsor, John H., an ex-Catholic Priest, guided me through the Big Book and several non-AA books on prayer and meditation that focused mostly on Eastern Spiritual practices.

In 1977 Joe and Charlie started their "Big Book Comes Alive" seminars and essentially changed all of AA's perspective of the Steps as worked from the first 164 pages of the Big Book. They were truly transforming and I believe that we owe those two guys nearly as much gratitude for their work as we do Bill and Dr. Bob. I told that to Charlie when I was the Saturday night speaker at one of their weekends, and he was very clear in his disagreement with that. He credited God's guidance and Bill's following God's guidance for the strength of the program. He insisted that he and Joe had simply sought that guidance in their studies of the Big Book and were passing it on to the rest of us. I am grateful to them.

In 1984, the General Service office of AA published the book "*Pass It On.*" In 1985, after Hughes moved the Apache

Helicopter Design Effort to Mesa, Arizona, I had read nearly this entire book. It seemed to me that it was a great AA History book and gave us a lot of background information about the development of our Program of Recovery.

On page 351 of *"Pass It On,"* it explains that Bill W. had about 15 years to watch people come into AA, work the 12 Steps from the Big book, get sober and remain sober, but also remain angry, anxious, depressed and filled with dread about their lives long after the high tide of active alcoholism had receded. It also explains that based on those observations he became convinced that it would be helpful to the fellowship if he wrote essays on each of the twelve steps and twelve traditions and published them under the title *"Twelve Steps and Twelve Traditions"* which over time became known simply as the "12 and 12." In a letter to his 'spiritual advisor' Father Dowling, dated July 17, 1952, he described the difficulty he found in "deepening and broadening" the Steps without changing them as they were initially written in the Big book. He explained the difficulty of finding the reasonable place to open and enter and at the same time avoid distortions and distractions that would surely arise from the diverse membership.

When I read this I took it to mean that Bill thought we should work each step in sequence, first from the Big Book, then deepen and broaden what we experienced by following the guidance on that Step in the 12 and 12. When I followed that guidance by working the Steps in 1985 I experienced my greatest period of growth.

Therefore, in following this guide, I suggest that you re-read each essay on each Step from the 12 and 12 before you use my interpretation and experience, so that you will also have Bill

W.'s language in mind when you are deepening and broadening your experience of the Step (after you have worked it from the Big Book.)

I will address this idea of "Broadening and Deepening" our experience of the Steps from the 12 and 12 as we go on through the 12 Steps.

Step One

§

"We admitted we were powerless over alcohol---
that our lives had become unmanageable."

I CAME INTO THE PROGRAM a full blown alcoholic with 39 years of baby elephant beliefs about life and living in the universe that had obviously not worked for me but at the time I could not see that. I thought that I was a victim of a bad father, a terrible childhood and an unlimited number of misfortunes and misunderstandings.

The straw that broke the camels back for me was that I had stolen some test equipment. I had done a lot of dumb things, but I had never stolen anything of real value in my life. Now I had and I felt like I was an immediate candidate for hard time in prison when I got caught. I knew I would never have stolen the equipment if I hadn't been drunk and I decided I needed to stop drinking for a while and get my act together, at least until I paid some debts and the equipment thing blew over.

At my first meeting, Chuck E., the member of the group having the longest sobriety, had explained the obsession to drink coupled with the physical reaction to the first drink that created a craving for another drink *which was much stronger than the alcoholic's will power not to drink*, I had stopped smoking on January 1, 1965, and I craved a cigarette worse than I had ever craved anything but my will power kept me from ever smoking another cigarette. I knew that I had never really craved a drink and I was sure that if I did my will power would overcome the desire to have another drink. My will power would allow me to drink just enough and then stop.

At the break I explained that to Kenny S., the guy who had brought me to my first meeting and came to be my first sponsor. He explained to me that I had never craved a cigarette until I had stopped smoking; and, that I had not craved a drink because I had obviously never stopped drinking once I started. I thought that was a very clever response but I didn't buy it.

The next Monday I went to San Diego to see about a side job to pay off debts that Pat didn't know we had, and I put myself to the test with a double shot of Old Crow. When we left the restaurant I wanted another drink. When we got to this guy's office I had to have a drink. When I could I slipped out and went to a liquor store and bought a half pint of Old Crow. It simply didn't occur to me to call on my will power to not have a drink. To borrow a metaphor from Joe and Charlie, my experience was that Willie Power didn't show up.

Once I got started I just kept drinking for the next four nights and days. I had never done that before, but I was on the streets of San Diego for four days and nights. My will power had simply not raised its powerful head one time to keep me from the next drink. I had not called home or called work. I was certain that I had lost my family and my job. I knew I was an alcoholic. I knew that I had to stop drinking. I wanted to stop drinking and I knew I could not stop without help. I told myself I am going to Alcoholics Anonymous to help me stop drinking. That was early Friday morning.

I bought a pint of whiskey and put it in my briefcase. The airports had just started looking into carry-on luggage. The security guy looked at my pint, looked at me, did that a couple times and then motioned me on. I flew back to LAX and went home. Pat was relieved to see me and was not immediately angry, just relieved. I took out my pint and told her that this was like my last cigarette. "When I finish this I am not going to drink again." She didn't want me to drink until I went to work to see if I still had a job. I went ahead and had a few drinks from that bottle and I took it with me in the car to work.

When I got to his office my boss had planned to fire me. He started to chew me out for missing the four days when I interrupted him and told him I was going to AA and that I wasn't going to drink again. He immediately changed his mind; he knew nothing about A.A. but its reputation was so attractive that he said to me: "Howard, I hope you do go to AA. I hope you don't ever drink again. I hope you don't break a leg, wreck your car, get polio, or anything else that will make you so much as late for work again. Furthermore, I don't want you to ever call in sick again. I want you to come in and I will tell you if you are sick or not. Do you understand me?" I understood, that, in a nut shell, was Tom's EAP program. I was very pleased not to lose my job and I was bound to be happy with everything that went with that.

He and I talked in his office for the next few hours. We stayed until after Security had locked the gate to his parking lot. He walked with me to my car and I drove him around the plant and into his parking lot and pulled up to his Cadillac. I put on my brakes and my pint bottle slid out from under his seat and rested between his feet. He looked at the bottle and then looked at me. Then he smiled and said "Let's finish this so you can stop drinking once and for all." He took a long drink and saved one for me. I took that drink and I have not had one since. That was August 4, 1972.

I was a long time in figuring this out, but I had taken the first part of the First Step on the sidewalks of San Diego early that morning on my way to the liquor store and the San Diego Airport. That surrender allowed the Spirit of the universe to smash my delusion that I could drink like other people.

You don't have to be the brightest bulb in the tree to see that working the Steps means you write down that you have stolen equipment, then you tell someone else you stole it, and then you take it back to where you stole it and say you're sorry. Well, that ain't going to happen with me. So I told my sponsor, Kenny, that I wasn't going to work the Steps and that I didn't believe God participated in our lives.

He wasn't upset by that and told me: "OK Howard, Let's make your entire A.A. Program for you to go to a meeting every night for 30 nights in a row. . . . In fact, we will go together." That last part turned out to be the catch because he added stuff to my program on our way to the meetings. Stuff like: "Listen close to what people are sharing and if something sounds like it would help you in your life, add that to your program."

I heard lots of stuff. Some of it I was able to take home and add to my program. For example, I heard a lady speaker say, "If you don't want to slip then don't go where it's slippery." I did not go into my old bar, The Tattle Tale Lounge, for years. And when I did it was in response to a sponsee's call for help.

However, most of the things I heard that sounded good to me, I could take home with high hopes, but when I tried to practice them the needed power wasn't there. Profound things such as: "If you make a mistake and brood about that, then you have made two mistakes; and, the brooding is generally the worst consequence of the first mistake." Another profound thought was: "All the people I hate do not feel the hate, but it is killing me." I took these things home but I couldn't stop brooding nor could I stop hating.

Although I did not actually see this for a long time into sobriety it became clear to me that the idea expressed on page 45 of the Big Book "We could wish to be moral, we could wish to be philosophically comforted, in fact we could will these things with all our might, but the needed power wasn't there."

Later I realized that what I was actually taking home from the meetings was hope. During my last years of drinking I didn't take much hope home from the Tattle Tale Lounge.

When I was about three months sober Kenny moved from Culver City to Simi Valley, about 50 miles away. I would drive out to see him some times but not more than once a week. I was going to meetings, helping Frank set up the home group meeting twice a week, then going to the after the meeting meetings with people having more time than me, and talking about the meeting over coffee or ice cream. Life was fun and getting better in sobriety. I was in Alcoholics Anonymous. Today I know that all of these actions help build new neural pathways necessary for a better life.

But occasionally, at work and at home, something would happen that scared me or angered me and I would think, "AA doesn't work. " Today I am convinced that my brain chemistry was the main source of that fear. I am also convinced that the things I was doing in AA were changing my brain chemistry, but it was happening slowly. Nevertheless, at that time when I was stressed out I would think "I am not going to drink but I am not going to those damn meetings either. We grin like baboons and tell each other how good life is and it isn't good and it isn't getting that much better. I am not going to the meeting tonight." But, when things cooled down I always went to the meetings.

One Saturday afternoon I was mowing the lawn. The lawnmower hit a tree root and I ran my chest into the bolt that held the lawn mower handle on. It hurt like blue blazes and I cried out: "God damn Pat anyway." Paused for another second and added: "Damn AA too." Now, if AA worked would my chest still hurt? I didn't think so. And once again I swore I was not going to another meeting. I wasn't going to drink but I wasn't going to a meeting either. That night I went to the Malibu meeting with a buddy I used to drink with in the Tattle Tale who came to AA after I did. On the way to the meeting we were grinning like baboons and telling each other how good AA worked.

One of my favorite speakers, a lawyer named Don G. was the main speaker. In his talk, he said: "If you are new in AA, or if you are an old-timer, and you are not working the Steps, AA will stop being fun and you will get to thinking that AA don't really work for you. Then you will think, I am not going to go to those meetings any longer; I am not going to drink, but I am not going to the meetings. Then you will decide to go the bar and have a drink. When you do that and the bartender asks, 'What's the matter? I thought you were going to AA. Doesn't AA work?' If you are not working the Steps be honest with the bartender and tell him, 'I don't know if AA would work or not, because I wouldn't try AA.'"

I heard that and it really made sense to me. You cannot know if AA works for you if you have not worked the Steps. On the way home I told my buddy, "I am going to work the Steps. Don is right; if you haven't worked the Steps you have not really tried AA."

With Kenny out of town I didn't really have an active sponsor, but I didn't want to get a new sponsor. I started to re-read the Big Book but as many of us do, I overlooked or misunderstood most of it. We have no idea how deep the baby elephant beliefs are buried. I was in nearly total denial about everything. I sometimes talked things over with Frank, but I was basically flying blind. Later, I was very slowly going to see that we are never flying blind if we are open to the next best thing.

One thing I was very clear on was the first part of the First Step: I was powerless over alcohol and I did not want to start drinking again. I saw that no matter how bad things got, drinking would only make them worse. For me drinking again would be *insane*. That conviction has remained with me for over 43 years of sobriety.

Part I, Step I: "We admitted we were powerless over alcohol---" Please keep in mind that the level of surrender we are able to experience that allows Grace to enter our lives and dispel the obsession to drink, disconnects the brain circuit from the drinking obsession; then creates circuits which progressively keep the "surrender "and the "don't take the first drink" circuits firing. Also keep in mind the "If we don't use it, we lose it" law.

There is no question about the importance of going to meetings and hearing over and over the horror stories of "taking the first drink," Including those that tell of successful prayers for help to not drink. Listening to stories about those prayers led me to the following experience with Frank.

I had essentially abandoned everything except panic praying when I got out of the service. After listening to a sober lady share about how prayer had taken away her obsession to drink I began to tell others that I did not believe that prayers worked. No one I explained that to seemed to care what I thought about prayer; some of these people simply gave me more examples of how prayer had worked for them. I could easily recognize the 'coincidences' involved in those experiences, but I didn't point these out because I didn't want to weaken their faith. If it works for them then "God bless them." But I had to live in the real world.

When I decided to discuss this issue with Frank, I explained to him that Dr. Einstein had once responded to a young girl in New York who had asked him if scientists pray. Einstein wrote her that scientist believed that everything happened in accordance with natural law and that a scientist would not believe that natural law could be influenced by a prayer which is a mere wish to a supernatural being .

"If Dr. Einstein doesn't believe in prayer I don't either," I told Frank. "I do not need any other authority."

Frank replied, "Well, I never learned to pray effectively until I learned to meditate."

"And just what is Meditation?" I asked.

"The best answer I have to that question is that Meditation for AA's is explained best in Step 11 of the 12 and 12."

"I have read that," I answered, "and it is about the St. Francis of Assisi Prayer, which is just what I am not going to do."

That statement led us to a visit with Frank and Lavon at their house the next Saturday morning. Frank and I were in their kitchen and Pat, our daughter Anne, and Lavon were in their living room. Frank and I read Step Eleven word by word, sentence by sentence, paragraph by paragraph from the 12 Steps and 12 Traditions.

It begins emphasizing that Step Eleven is what Step Eleven says it is: Seeking through pray and meditation to improve our conscious contact with God.

Frank said to me, "If you believe there is a God then perhaps it may be possible to be in contact with Him. In which case you would not want to skip the principle method that AA has in being in contact with God? . . Why that would really be practicing the principle of '. . . contempt prior to investigation.'"

"Maybe so," I answered, "but what is meditation? How do you do it?"

Frank paused, his eyes smiling, and patiently added, "I will get into that in just a moment. But I want to emphasize that Bill W. knew the meaning of every word he used; and he was a good enough writer to put those words in an understandable context. When you are reading Bill W.'s writings pay close attention to his use of words and don't be afraid to look words up in a dictionary. I don't believe a special dictionary is required.

Use your current Webster's if you wish. But I recommend that you use it. You may be reading Bill's writings for a long time and it is important to understand what he is saying."

Pausing again to take a sip of coffee, he then added: "In a letter to an AA member written in 1946 Bill W. wrote something to the affect that our defects stand between us and the sunlight of the Spirit. So, our blindness is the result of our defects and we must first deeply realize within our inner most self what they are. Constructive mediation is the first requirement for each new Step in our spiritual growth."

That information, coupled with my subsequent experience, is among the most important elements of my spiritual practice.

"Now," Frank continued, "My answer to your question "What is meditation?" the way I read the 12 and 12, meditation is being conscious of what you want to be conscious of. Bill uses the St. Francis of Assisi Prayer and being conscious of the deeper meaning of each phrase, word and idea in the Prayer." Frank explained, not smiling, which is his typical expression. "Let's look at what Bill says about it."

"Basically he tells us that meditation is being conscious of what we want to be conscious of; logically interwoven with our awareness of how our life fits with the deepest meaning of this consciousness and then aligning that into your life through prayer forms an unshakeable foundation on which our lives can be built." Frank pauses again, and then goes on "Do you think your life is on an unshakeable base right now?"

"No! You know I do not think that." I told him.

"Then you don't want to skip the practice of prayer and meditation, do you?" Frank emphasized.

"Okay, Frank. I have tried Prayer since I was a little kid and I never felt like it was helpful to me. But, I have never tried to meditate and logically interrelating that with prayer and I am willing to give it a try. But I don't understand how to go about that from reading the 12 and 12."

"Rather than trying to explain what and how to do meditation I will demonstrate the process for you with a guided meditation. Now Bill W. has suggested that we start with the St. Francis Prayer, but I don't want us to do that. After all, that is a saint's prayer and we aren't saints." His eyes indicted that he was smiling but his mouth was still curved downwards. "This guided meditation will be on the First Step from the language in the Big Book. I will quote passages that refer to the first part of the First Step. As we go through the Big Book description of the alcoholic and alcoholic behavior, play close attention to the deeper meaning of each word and phrase. We will call that meditation. Then, when we have finished those descriptions we will pause and be conscious of whether we see that our experience with alcohol and alcoholism fits the Big Book descriptions. If we see that our experiences fit those descriptions then we will call that self-examination."

I had followed him pretty well this far, "Then how do we logically interrelate and interweave meditation and self-examination into prayer?" I insisted.

"First things first, Howard, and first let's interrelate and interweave meditation and self-examination and then we will connect it with prayer."

I hope those readers who have stayed with me this far will follow along with Frank and me through this next experience.

He had me get comfortably seated, with my back and neck in alignment and being awake but relaxed. He had me follow along with his quotations from the Big Book that describes the alcoholic and alcoholic thinking and behavior. "Listen carefully for the deeper meaning of each word and phrase," he told me.

After a few seconds of quiet breathing he began with the First Step, repeating it all from memory from the Big Book: "Step One: We admitted we were powerless over alcohol—that our lives had become unmanageable."

After a short pause he said "We will now repeat the First Step several times very slowly, listening for the deeper meaning of each word and idea.

We did that, and he followed that with the following: "Now let's follow along in the Big Book and go through Part one of Step One:" . . . "We admitted we were powerless over alcohol. The Big Book then tells us that 'Alcoholics are men and women who have lost the ability to control their drinking. . . .'

Then he went deeper. "The loss of control is characterized by an insane obsession that somehow, someway, this time I am going to drink just enough to feel good and no more, this time it is going to be different." . . . "But then we are told that coupled with that insane obsession to take the first drink is a physical reaction to alcohol which manifests in a phenomenon of craving for more alcohol once we start to drink. That this phenomenon of craving is limited to this class and never occurs in the average temperate drinker." . . . "We are restless, irritable and discontented, unless we can again experience the sense of ease and comfort which comes at once by taking a few drinks---drinks which their insane obsession convinces them they can take with impunity. After they have succumbed to the desire again, as so many do, and the phenomenon of craving develops, they pass through the well know stages of a spree, emerging remorseful, with a firm resolution not to drink again. This is repeated over and over; and, over any considerable period of time it gets worse never better. Which leads in time to pitiful and incomprehensible demoralization?"

"Now," Frank went on, "If you were able to follow along with these descriptions of the alcoholic and alcoholic behavior, we will call that meditation, and if you are conscious that your experience with alcohol fits those descriptions, we will call that self-examination. Then you pause to 'fully concede to your innermost self that you are an alcoholic.' That, the Big Book tells us is our First Step in recovery."

Following a long pause, Frank added, "While we are in touch with our innermost selves, let's also concede that if we drink again we will almost immediately return to pitiful and Incomprehensible demoralization."

"Now sit quietly for a few more minutes and be open to being conscious of how much your life has changed for the better since you have come to AA; and be aware of how little you did to bring that about. That better things just seemed to happen when you are not drinking; and that you could not stop drinking without coming to AA."

In a few moments I felt a sense of well-being just from staying sober since the fourth of August. Then, I asked Frank "How about prayer. How does that fit in?"

"Well, Howard, if you felt pleasure after that guided meditation, we will call that feeling 'gratitude,' which the dictionary defines as 'something affording pleasure by reason of comfort supplied or discomfort removed.' One prayer might simply be: "Thank you, God."

"But," he quickly added, "I do not want you to pray that way. "Thank you, God" is just words. If you feel gratitude, don't stop that to say words, just feel the gratitude. Let that be your prayer." . . . If you do that you will occasionally have a very good feeling start at just above the ankles and come up your entire body, leaving goose bumps on the back of your hands and neck. When that happens I want you to know: That is my God saying: 'Howard, I felt your gratitude and you are welcome.'"

Frank and I talked for a while longer. I had a feeling that this was life changing for me, but I had no idea the extent of that change. Frank went on to tell me to extend my experience with working the Steps on through all of the Steps so that I could deepen my experience of the Steps within my innermost self.

I tried to express my gratitude to him for his help that morning, but he was right about just saying words when you say "Thank you, Frank." But somehow that morning I knew that Frank felt my gratitude at a much deeper spiritual level than mere words.

That morning with Frank and the 12 and 12 resulted in my reading with a greater openness to being conscious of the deeper meaning of whatever I was reading; and to be open to experiencing my level of identification with what I was reading. Why not give that a try while you are reading the following ideas taken from the Big Book and the 12 and 12?

The Big Book asks: "But what about the real alcoholic? He may start off as a moderate drinker; he may or may not become a continuous hard drinker; but at some stage of his drinking career he begins to lose all control of his liquor consumption, once he starts to drink." Page 21, Big Book

"We alcoholics are men and women who have lost the ability to control our drinking." Page 30, Big Book

"The idea that somehow, someday he will control and enjoy his drinking is the great obsession of every abnormal drinker." Page 30, Big Book

Coupled with this insane obsession, all alcoholics, ". . . have one symptom in common: they cannot start drinking without developing the phenomenon of craving. . . . which differentiates these people, and sets them apart as a distinct entity?" Page xxviii, Big Book

Alcoholics ". . . are restless, irritable and discontented, unless they can again experience the sense of ease and comfort which comes at once by taking a few drinks---drinks which their insane obsession convinces them they can take with impunity. After they have succumbed to the desire again, as so many do, and the phenomenon of craving develops, they pass through the well-known stages of a spree, emerging remorseful, with a firm resolution not to drink again. This is repeated over, and over any considerable period of time it gets worse never better." Page xxvii, Big Book

"All of us felt at times that we were regaining control, but such intervals---usually brief---were inevitably followed by still less control, which led in time to pitiful and incomprehensible demoralization. . . . "We learned we had to fully concede to our innermost selves that we were alcoholics. This is the first step in recovery." Page 30, Big Book

I think that Bill W.'s spiritual experience at Towne's Hospital, and the events that followed that experience were crucial in the subsequent formation of the Alcoholics Anonymous program. In the Oxford Group such spiritual experiences were "checked" by more experienced members in an effort to validate them. In Bill's case Ebby was selected to do this. After seeing the change that this experience had brought about in Bill, Ebby did not feel qualified to check Bill's experience. Instead, Ebby gave Bill a copy of Williams James's book "*The Variety of Religious Experiences*," for Bill to read in an effort to check his experience himself.

Anyone who has read James's book knows that it is a tough book to read. But Bill started reading it as soon as Ebby left his hospital room and he devoured in from cover to cover while still in the hospital. As noted on page 124 of "*Pass It On*," Bill was able to discern that all of the stories in Doctor James' book shared three common denominators: First, each person had been completely defeated in some circumstance and event of his life; Second, each person had surrendered to the fact that he was defeated; and, Third, each person had asked for help, not always for religious help but help from a source they recognized as having the power to help.

My experience on the streets of San Diego the morning of August 4, 1972 was exactly that experience; although my corresponding spiritual awakening was very much a gradual experience rather than a "sudden spectacular" one. Bill's descriptions early in Step Six of the 12 and 12, of alcoholics who drink so much alcohol that they destroy their lives are actually working against nature's law of self -preservation. He also noted that this level of defeat is necessary for the individual to experience the humility that allows God to smash their delusion that they can drink like normal people. I think Bill makes it clear that he believes that God will not remove our delusions unless we surrender them at that level. I believe that without that happening I may have never stopped drinking. For myself, re-experiencing that "pitiful and incomprehensible demoralization" through working the first part of the first step as described above, has cemented that God given change into my inner most self.

Also, "obsessions of the mind," are made up of very active neural circuits energizing and driving the obsession. Chuck C. identified these obsessions as "children of the ego." Fighting my ego is clearly a losing battle; as long as I fight to change my ego's obsession it will continue to be engaged.

Be conscious of the language Bill has used: ". . . fully concede to our innermost selves that we are alcoholic." Be as conscious as possible of the deeper meaning of each word and phrase. This not only insures that we reach our innermost selves with our concession that we are an alcoholic; but it enables us to experience who we really are. The deeper meaning of each word and phrase might be considered part of the ego's ". . . set of thoughts that define your universe. . ." But 'your inner most self' is who you are. You are the being that is conscious of the presence of the Spirit within you. It is in our innermost self where we convert the thought prison into our living room. Quietly settle into the consciousness of that truth about yourself. Now, know in your deepest self that you, in and of yourself, are powerless to not drink and know that you need help and that you came to AA to find that help.

Now, being conscious of what an alcoholic is and does; and your admission that you are an alcoholic, fully concede to your innermost self that if you drink or use again you will almost immediately return to pitiful and incomprehensible demoralization. That is a principle we need to practice in all of the Twelve Steps, but especially in the First. The First Step is the first stone in the unshakeable foundation we are building our sober lives on. Settle into that consciousness for a few minutes.

Also, consider this. When we stop drinking and using we are giving our brain centers a chance to heal themselves of all the 'burn' damage caused by our earlier full time drinking. Nothing can get better for us until we stop drinking and using.

As I have noted several times earlier my spiritual growth was slow and I was 13 years sober before I was open to God's presence in my life. Nevertheless, when I first started working the first Step my behavior changed. While I had been unsuccessful in trying to stop brooding and hating, after I started the Steps I found that I was brooding and hating less and that this came about without my making a conscious effort to make those changes.

PART 2, STEP 1: "---THAT OUR LIVES HAD BECOME UNMANAGEABLE."
When I first read this part of Step One it was immediately clear to me that it was true that our lives had become unmanageable when we were drunk. Certainly our lives had become unmanageable. But now that we were sober we had to and could manage our lives.

Once again, our culture teaches us that we must be individual achievers. That we must win the competition; that competition is the greatest thing since sliced bread. We are told that we must win the competition and become the best, or the boss, and with that we will have money, property and prestige, which will in turn be the basis for us to experience a sense of well-being.

With our brain chemistry we are spring loaded to fight and flight; anger and fear. Also, being a quart low in dopamine and serotonin our pleasure centers are difficult to activate. That particular combination means we are shoveling sand (or whatever it is we are shoveling) against the tide. The last thing you want is to feel is pleasure when facing a grizzly or when responding to the ego's grizzly. At times, our brains do not clearly distinguish between a threat to our life and a threat to our ego; all threats to the ego are grizzles to many alcoholics.

The guy in my home group that had the second longest length of sobriety was named Leo H. I think he had 23 years when I heard him say "You newcomers need to stay away from those middle steps. Especially that Fourth Step; if you get into that Fourth Step too soon it will get you drunk rather than keep you sober. I have found and maintained a wonderful way of life for 23 years just working the First and the Twelfth Steps. If you work those two Steps you will automatically work the other Steps as much as you need to." That made perfect sense to me.

Early in my sobriety I understood that in doing the Fourth Step I was going to have to write down that I had stolen the test equipment. Then I was going to have to tell that "to another human being;" and in the Ninth Step I was going to have to return the test equipment. As quickly as I understood those things I also understood that I was not going to work those Steps. I am going to follow Leo's advice and stick with the First and Twelfth Steps. Years later I learned that my sponsor Kenny had also been following Leo's advice and he didn't work the other Steps until he was 13 years sober and some guy molested his granddaughter. He later told me that he found that he was going to have to forgive the guy or kill him so he worked his way through all the Steps and forgave him.

When I was sober about five weeks I had been going to meetings every night. Pat was beginning to complain that I wasn't home as much now as I had been when I was drinking. When I came home from work that Friday she was angry and I thought she was being unreasonable. After all, I had been sober for nearly six weeks and I thought she should be giving more strokes for that. As soon as dinner was over I went to the Friday night speaker's meeting.

I got there a little early and Frank, who was the Group Secretary, was having trouble with the building lights. When it started to get a little dark I decided to set up the tables and chairs for the meeting. Those were the heaviest tables I had ever lifted. "Why is this old man putting these tables up without any help?" I wondered. By the time I had the tables and chairs set up Frank had the lights on, the coffee made and the literature out.

The speaker's meeting had a short speaker, birthday cakes, a coffee break and a main speaker. Following the main speaker Frank always closed the meeting with announcements, and then led us into the Lord's Prayer by saying, "I know God will manifest everything I really believe, and I really believe in Alcoholics Anonymous." Then everyone in the room gathered in a big circle, held hands and prayed the Lord's Prayer.

That night, when Frank was making the announcements, he looked me right in the eye and I knew he was going to tell the group that I had come early and had set up the tables and chairs. And, I wanted him to do that; I wanted everyone to know about my helping out. Frank then averted his eyes and said his "I believe . . . "thing and we joined up and said the Lord's Prayer. He had not thanked me. "Well, damn him anyway." I thought. "Let the old son-of-a-bitch put the tables up himself."

All the men always jumped right in to tear the meeting down, putting those heavy tables in a slide under the stage and the chairs in racks in the closet. We were done in a flash.

I was still angry about Frank not thanking me when he took me aside and said, "Howard, I almost screwed it up for you."

"What do you mean, almost screwed it up?"

Looking me straight in the eyes he said, "I almost thanked you from the podium for helping with the tables and chairs. But I realized that you would want to have done that anonymously."

I hadn't even thought of doing it anonymously, but I got the message.

That exchange was the basis for a major transformation in me: Doing something for someone else without expecting anything in return.

Frank and I set both the beginner's and speaker's meeting up together anonymously for the next four years when Frank passed on from esophageal cancer. During that first year and after, he took me with him on Twelve Step calls, to CSR and GSR meetings; we answered the central office phones together for the first shift on Saturday nights and he taught me to meditate and pray in a very special way. What a teacher. . . And he was not my only teacher; my life was full of teachers. Some had many years on the program and some only a few months or a few years, but they were all old-timers to me.

The point here is that for the first time in my life I was doing things in an effort to help other people; and I was doing it for fun and for free. As Bill W. notes in Appendix II of the Big Book, the ". . . friends of the newcomer are aware of the difference long before he is himself. . . . What often takes place in a few months could seldom have been accomplished by years of self-discipline." My work life and home life remained stressful, but less so than before, but my life in A.A. was becoming better than I could have dreamed it would be.

Before Kenny had decided to move to Simi Valley, he came home with me and talked Pat into giving Al-Anon a try. She and I both thought she didn't need to go to Al-Anon because I wasn't drinking. But, she and I continued to have trouble and she was getting sick of my sober behavior. I didn't know what was wrong with her but I knew I couldn't please her with anything I did.

As time went on I was being invited to speak at meetings. In the fall of 1974 the Southern California Convention Committee decided to have a Saturday midnight speaker meeting with two sober AA's having under five years. I was invited to be the second speaker. It was a big honor and I actually felt humble about being asked. After that, mostly because the committee taped that talk and the taper sent it out to other meetings, I was getting more invitations to speak out of town. I insisted that Pat go with me. At first she didn't complain or argue, but as time went on and the drives got longer she started to drag her feet about going. We had been invited to go from Los Angles to Fresno and she went with me. After I talked at their meeting they put Pat and I up in a motel and we saw the sights in Fresno and drove home Sunday afternoon. We had a great time.

Some months later I got another invitation to speak in Fresno and Pat immediately said she didn't want to go to Fresno again. That didn't worry me because she always caved in and went with me when I insisted that she should go. On the Friday morning before the Saturday I was scheduled to speak in Fresno I reminded Pat that we were driving to Fresno tomorrow. She responded with "Honey, I told you I didn't want to go with you this time; that you should take one of your sponsees."

"Now listen to me Pat," I told her starting my sales pitch. "We never say no to a legitimate AA request, and while I may not be a great speaker I was invited and I have committed to go. I need you to go along and keep me company and we will have a great time together."

Pat looked me in the eye, smiling pleasantly and said, "Howard, you know I love you; and we are going to be together forever. And, if it causes you pain for me not to go to Fresno with you," pausing to take a deep breath she added, "I want you to know that I love you enough to help you go through the pain. But I am not going to go to Fresno with you."

It wasn't so bad that she didn't go to Fresno with me. I took one of my sponsees and I talked all the way to Fresno, all the time in Fresno and all the way home. I had a great time.

But Pat had experienced something new in her life. Al-Anon had somehow taught her that she didn't have to do everything I wanted her to and that I would stay sober. When I argued that "We are married, god damn it, and married people as supposed to do things together." She would not get angry and would respond calmly, "We do lots of things together, but I am not going to do this with you."

"Why not?" I would ask.

"I don't have a really good reason; your reasons are always better than mine. But my basic reason is that I do not want to go this time. I guess that no simply has to be the complete answer." And she said it so sweetly.

I had no idea how often I had insisted on having my way and that Pat had caved in to me just to get along. It was truly a shock to my system to encounter this new attitude and behavior.

When I was finishing my first Fourth Step, a guy named George C. kept asking me how I was coming along with it. George's family was in the acting business and George had become an "also-starring" movie actor in the late 50's. He had drifted somehow into the technical publication business with the NASA buildup of the space program and he had a successful Tech Pub company. George had drunk his way down the tubes, like many do, and he had come to AA through a nudge from the judge. He had a year or so more sobriety than I had and he was busy as a bit part actor, male model, an engineering company employee, and helping newer people get sober. The latter work assignment seemed to be pretty much focused on me and my progress on the Fourth Step. He was becoming a pain in the ass about it.

As I mentioned earlier Kenny had moved to Simi Valley, California earlier in my sobriety. I would drive out to see him almost weekly, but I went to meetings on the west side of Los Angeles nearly every night and while becoming a pain in the ass, George also became my friend. I had asked George to hear my Fifth Step and after I had shared my secrets with him I wanted to ensure his confidentiality by asking him to be my sponsor. When it seemed to me that Al-Anon had made Pat completely unreasonable I went to George and complained to him about her changing behavior.

George heard me out and then said to me, "It sounds like we need another trip through the 12 Steps."

"Boy that is the truth, except I am not sure she has gone through them the first time." I quickly replied.

George laughed and said, "No, Howard. I don't mean Pat needs to go through the Steps again; I mean you need to go through the Steps again."

I could not believe that he was saying that to me. I thought, "What the hell did I ask an actor to be my sponsor for? Actors don't know anything about real life. He is just saying "You need to work the Steps again because he doesn't really know anything."

"Well Howard," he said. "You did a great job when you worked them the first time. Especially when you didn't really have anyone to help you go through them. You did them well and it changed your life. But now you are having problems with

Pat, and it seems to me that she may be being reasonable about this. Why don't we go through the Steps together using the Big Book?"

George didn't know what the hell he was saying but I decided to humor him and at least agree to work the Fourth Step again. When I suggested that he responded "I have heard you share on the First part of the First Step and I agree that you don't have to take that over again. But I think we should look at the unmanageability of your life in the First Step when you are having this trouble with Pat. Why don't we start there?

It is amazing to me that Bill W. knew very little about the chemical and mental differences of the alcoholic, but described the actions taken through the Steps in a precise sequence and in increments that directly and effectively address those differences.

"Our liquor was but a symptom." Page 64, Big Book

"The first requirement is that we be convinced that any life run on self-will can hardly be a success." . . . "Each person is like an actor who wants to run the whole show; is forever trying to arrange the lights, the ballet, the scenery and the rest of the players in his own way. If his arrangements would only stay put, if only people would do as he wished the show would be great. Everybody, including himself would be pleased. Life would be wonderful. In trying to make these arrangements our actor may sometimes be quite virtuous. He may be kind, considerate, patient, generous and self-sacrificing. On the other hand, he may be mean, egotistical, selfish and dishonest. . . . The show doesn't come off very well. . . . He becomes . . . still more demanding or gracious, as the case may be." . . . "He becomes angry, indignant, self-pitying. What is his basic trouble? . . . Is he not the victim of the delusion that he can wrest satisfaction and happiness out of this world if he only manages well?" Page 60-61, Big Book.

Now, once again we might slowly re-read the second part of the First Step description of your selfishness and self-centeredness, taking in the deep meaning of each phrase and idea. At the same time be conscious of how well that description of self-centeredness fits your own behavior. Then, be conscious of your most recent difficulty in life and see how that was a manifestation of your not having your way. Know that there are no other causes of problems, difficulties, or unresolved circumstances in your life. Settle into the consciousness of your inability to manage your life so that you will be free of problems and difficulties. Fighting to have our way so we can be happy and satisfied can never successfully happen. Again, if we are going to be able to stop this fight we need to experience "deflation at depth," to a level much deeper than our intellect, and as humble as we can be we ask for help, and help will be there. In a slightly more subtle way, when we ask for help we are at the same time finding hope. If we didn't have hope we would not be asking for help.

"And we have ceased fighting anything or anyone---even alcohol." Page 84, Big Book

"Besides, we have stopped fighting anybody or anything." Page 103, Big Book

Think about that for a moment; when we actually stop fighting anything or anyone---even alcohol. . ." we will be shutting off neural transmitters that activate the fight or flight center of our brain. Remember the Second Principle of Neuro Plasticity: "If you don't use it you lose it."

This second iteration with the Steps started in the middle of my second year. I subsequently went through the Steps again in 1975 when I was promoted back into management at work. In retrospect I can see that the fact that I wanted to become less selfish with Pat created a new level of stress in my life. As George suggested, I need to work the Steps to do that. Similarly, my promotion back into management created a level of stress that required me to go through the Steps again. This time with my third sponsor, John H., who had spent the past twenty years drinking himself out of the Priesthood.

PART 3, STEP 1.

On Page 11 of the Big Book, when Bill was expressing his doubts about God being of much help, he declared: "But my friend sat before me, and he made the pointblank declaration that God had done for him what he could not do for himself." . . ."Had this power originated in him? Obviously it had not. There had been no more power in him than there was in me at that minute; and this was none at all."

Later in the hospital, on Page 13, Bill stated: "I admitted for the first time that of myself I was nothing; that without Him I was lost."

Now in order to look for ways Bill had deepened and broadened the First Step "in the lives of newcomers and oldtimers alike" (as promised in his letter to Father Dowling in '*Pass It On*) let's take a look at Step One in the 12 and 12. As suggested earlier, you would benefit a great deal from reading that essay now.

You will notice that on the first page of the 12 and 12's description of the First Step Bill explains that it is only natural for an alcoholic to argue against the idea that he has no personal power at all. Then, in the third paragraph of that page Bill insists that by admitting that we have no personal power we are establishing a foundation upon which comfortable and happy lives could be built.

When it dawned on me that Bill might mean just what he said, that I have no personal power, I clearly doubted that. And, in that point of my sobriety, when I saw that I was agitated or doubtful about something I would schedule a time for meditation where I would be conscious of what I doubted and would then be open to being given an answer.

When that occurred to me my immediate answer was "Of course it doesn't mean actual 'personal powerlessness,' because I am not actually 'personally powerless.' "

I personally have the power to decide to pick up the Big Book," I thought, I just don't have much power. "Having decided to pick it up I have the power to take it in my hands and pick it up. Therefore I am not personally powerless."

In a few seconds the thought came to me, "That's right, Howard. Now wrap your vision around it and pick it up with your vision. . . . Levitate it up."

"I don't have that power." I responded.

Then the thought, "Well, give yourself that power."

"I can't give myself that power. That is silly."

There was a pause and then my next thought was: "No, you can't. And you did not give yourself the power to decide to pick the book up with your hands; and you did not give yourself the power to pick it up with your hands. Whatever power you do have has come to you from some other source of power. . . . In and of yourself, *you are personally powerless.*"

Then, I considered that truth. Whatever power I do have, that power had to be given to me by some other source of power. I cannot give power to myself. Then, I settled into the consciousness of that truth and became open to its deeper meanings.

Finally, I fully conceded to my innermost self that I am an alcoholic; that I cannot manage the outcome of the events of my life so that I can experience happiness and satisfaction (That is an insane delusion); and know that in and of myself I am personally powerless. On that *foundation* I can build a happy and productive life. Surrendering at that level I found I was much less likely to keep fighting to have things come out my way; and more willing to accept things that I have not been given the power to change. When I meditate and pray in this manner every morning I am building neural pathways that gradually changed my thinking from my getting what I want, to wanting what I was getting. This change is slow but it is relentless.

That experience was a powerful demonstration in my life of what Bill had written in the 1946 letter Frank had told me about: "Constructive meditation is the first requirement for each new step in our spiritual progress."

However, I am convinced that these spiritual practices must be experienced in combination with all the 12 Steps, taken in their specific sequence and increments.

I also think it is important to make note of another recommendation Bill has included in Step One of the 12 and 12. Throughout the 12 and 12 Bill emphasized that an alcoholic's recovery is contingent on their admissions that their lives have become unmanageable. He also notes that many new people are much younger than the average member when the program was first started; and that some were little more than heavy drinkers. He questions how those new members would be able to see their plight at a level needed for the required surrender. Bill's idea on this issue makes a great deal of sense, especially today when so many young people who are still in their teens and early 20's, are coming into the program. Bill's idea was to make it clear that alcoholics may or may not become serious heavy drinkers, but if they are alcoholic, at some point they will begin to lose control. That those of us who have gone farther down the road of alcoholism would be helpful to the new members if we would go back through our drinking history and relate the control problems that we had in our early drinking days. How those problems got progressively worse never better, as we progressed in our alcoholism. Then, if these younger people go back out for more drinking they will recognize that they are on that same alcoholic path to destruction and will be able to surrender at a level that is needed for Grace to enter their lives and smash the delusion that they can drink like normal people.

Step Two

§

"Came to believe that a power greater than ourselves could return us to sanity."

IN HIS BOOK "*THE PERENNIAL Philosophy*," Aldous Huxley included an essay on Faith. In it he described religious faith as an act of will where a person intellectually assents that a proposition is true when the person knows he can not verify the truth of the proposition in this lifetime. Examples he offers of this religious faith are the doctrine of the Immaculate Conception and much of the Apostles Creed. He doesn't argue that these doctrines are untrue, he only argues that faith in such propositions must be intellectually willed, and that such faith is only found in religions.

I had met my wife Pat when we were in the seventh grade. She was my girlfriend for a short time that summer but I was prone to getting into trouble and she did not want to get into trouble. She soon stopped being my girlfriend but remained my friend throughout elementary and high school where we graduated together. I never told her that I loved her but secretly she was my dream girl. While in the service I heard that she was engaged to a guy I didn't like and my heart was broken. I had decided not to go home on leave because I didn't want to be there if she was married to that guy. Then I heard that she had 'dumped' him and I decided to go home and tell her that I loved her. It turned out that we had a great time together while I was on leave. We went dancing and to movies and I did tell her that I was in love with her and had always loved her. "I am not proposing or anything, but I wanted to tell you that I loved you and ask you if we can stay in touch when I go back to the ship." She agreed and after I returned to duty we frequently wrote each other.

In the navy I had met a lot of Catholics guys and I was impressed with how well they understood Catholic doctrine and the basis for believing what they were taught. I was much impressed with the Instructions of the Catholic Church and I decided to be baptized.

I wrote Pat a love letter and proposed to her that we get married. I told her I was taking Instructions in the Catholic Church and that we would be married in the Church and that our children would have to be raised Catholic. In retrospect I think that I took that approach so that when she refused to marry me I could argue to myself that she wasn't rejecting me she was rejecting the Catholic Church. Much to my surprise and elation, she responded by telling me she would love to marry me and she would love to have my children, but "I could never marry you in the Catholic Church. If I did I would be disowned by my entire family."

My interest in becoming a Catholic immediately went to zero. Patty Ingram would love to marry me and she would love to have my children. Nothing could be better than that. We were married in San Diego, California on September 22, 1953, and I was honorably discharged from the U.S. Navy on October 27, 1953. Our son Timothy was born on August 16, 1954. As I described earlier, I was nearly immobilized with anxiety and was soon on my way to becoming an alcoholic.

After Pat and I were married I lost interest in Christianity. While attending Wichita University in 1954, my youngest sister had told me that Dr. Einstein was an atheist and I had thought that if he is an atheist I would be an atheist too. Then, I was reading the book *"The World as I See It,"* by Dr. Einstein wherein he declared himself to be a "deeply religious man." Well, I thought, if Dr. Einstein is not an atheist I am not an atheist either. Later, I read somewhere that Dr. Einstein was a practicing deist.

In the 17th and 18th centuries the implications of Newton's laws for a "clockwork universe" had resulted in a movement called deism. Although all of its proponents did not follow the same path, deism generally defended the reasonableness of religion and a belief in God. This teaching proposed that God had initiated creation of the universe and imbued that creation with immutable laws to govern the universe. This Creator had then allowed creation to follow its own course without the intervention of miracles. These immutable laws of the causal system led Dr. Einstein to declare "The future, (to the scientist) is every whit as necessary and determined as the past."

But to my knowledge Dr. Einstein never described himself as believing in any particular religious philosophy, arguing that it was too mystical and complex for the human mind to grasp.

For my own part, I decided that I would be a deist and that was the religious system I brought with me into the AA Program. In general I was convinced of the existence of immutable laws that governed everything in the universe. If man wanted to learn to fly he would have to understand the laws of aerodynamics and how to engage them with a dynamic airfoil and in that way he could actually fly. And, so it was for everything in the universe.

That also meant that if I was going to be successful as an engineer I was going to have to not only learn the immutable laws of engineering, but I was going to also have to learn the laws that man had created to be successful in a business organization and how to conform to those laws.

I need to emphasize that I didn't have that clear of an idea of what I was actually trying to do, but I can assure you that it all depended on me getting things done myself. Coupled with that unclear religious belief was a lifetime full of baby elephant beliefs that I was not conscious that I had. Obviously, this was an extremely stressful approach to reaching the goals in life.

As I described earlier, gradually, through my experiences in the Program I came to believe that the immutable laws for sobriety and a happy and comfortable life for alcoholics were in the Steps and the Traditions. I believed that Bill W., Doctor Bob, and the other founders of AA had the intelligence, connections and spiritual insights to actually create this Program and describe 'How It Works.'

As I also described earlier I attended many meetings and became a good listener. Although my head "popped off" in disbelief at much of what I heard, I also heard many common sense spiritual principles that I "Came to Believe" and which improved the quality of my life. I had exceptionally good sponsors and others working with me and helping me into the Program. In general each new sponsor was the perfect guy for my life at that time and place in my life.

While I was very slow to become open to the possible existence of God being active in my life, I was not totally blind to how many major improvements in the quality of my life were connected to "amazing coincidences." Things like my sponsor having been a high school chum of the fence that I had given the stolen test equipment to and how "lucky" I had been to return the equipment before Security even discovered it was missing.

On page 8 of the Big Book Bill W. encouraged those seeking a spiritual awakening that there were many helpful books outside of AA approved literature. (As AA historian Mike Fitzpatrick once explained to me: "AA does not have a list of conference disapproved literature"). In addition, Bill made encouraging references to turning to science to find a Higher Power.

It seems to me that Bill's primary approach was to "Come to Believe" in whatever way you were able to do that. At the start of the second half of my first AA meeting on July 26, 1972, someone read Pages 92 and 93 from the Big Book: "Even though your protégé may not have entirely admitted his condition, he has become very curious to know how you got well. Let him ask you that question, if he will. Tell him exactly what happened to you. Stress the spiritual feature freely. If the man be agnostic or atheist, make it emphatic that he does not have to agree with your conception of God. He can choose any conception he likes, provided it makes sense to him." That had a very powerful effect on me: "Provided it makes sense to him." That was going to be my criteria in finding my "Higher Power."

My early efforts at trying to will myself to ascent that unverifiable truths were true, which I then got tangled up with the verifiable truths taught in religion and science and most of it didn't make sense to me. Hence, I abandoned as many of my early religious teaching as I could and simply started over. In doing that I (at least temporarily) threw the baby out with the bath water.

The keys to my gradual changing belief system were that I committed to attend meetings, I always had the "right" sponsor, that I actively maintained a practice of daily meditation and prayer, and that I successfully worked through the Steps during times of extreme stress in sobriety.

I had read an article on the practice of deism that stated that "spiritual insights" experienced while meditating were basically insights coming from our intellect rather than from a spiritual source. That made perfect sense to me. I was convinced that drinking alcohol had actually enabled me to access my intellect so that I could write technical reports and complete detailed analysis of technical problems. It made sense that quieting my stress filled mind with meditation provided relief that allowed my intellect to consider work issues instead of anxious and angry thoughts that resulted in the immobilizing stress.

A major turning point in my coming to believe in the pervasive presence and Power of the Spirit of God being active in my life happened in my 13th year of sobriety. In 1985 I was promoted to the position of Technical Section Manager in the

Systems Engineering Department of the Helicopter Design Division and was given what amounted to a 30 percent pay increase. The position of Technical Section Manager was my career goal and I was very excited about that. There was however, a "Baby Elephant Belief" I didn't realize I had associated with this promotion. That belief was that it was stressful to work your way up to your career goal, but once you had reached that goal the stressful part of life would be over.

Two days after I received the promotion my boss gave me an assignment to make a presentation to a 2 star general who was the army's program manager on the Apache Helicopter. This presentation was a status report on the technical, schedule and budgetary position of a complex computer oriented data system for the first production helicopters. The General, his Technical Staff and three Ph.D. Physicists from John Hopkins University who were expert in these systems would attend the presentation and advise the General if the system would be adequately developed to justify a recommendation to go into Production. I did not believe I was qualified to make this presentation and my boss felt like my recent promotion required me to make it.

The first few minutes of my meditation the next morning was simply experiencing the dread of risking my entire career in my first assignment as a section manager, and failing and never recovering from the failure. Then I was able to disengage from that stressful thought process and engage in my meditation. When my timer went off I felt relaxed and felt a sense of well-being. I didn't back out of my meditation, however, because I knew I would back out into the dreadfulness of that assignment.

I then asked "Why do I have to meditate in order to function. My boss doesn't meditate, his boss doesn't meditate. Why me?" Then, as if an answer to those questions in my mind's eye I saw a frozen lake. I knew that the ice on this lake was as thick as the laws of physics will allow ice to get. I knew that you could put a Sherman Tank on that ice and it would be supported.

Then this thought, as if spoken by the voice, came to me: "Walking across the frozen lake a step at a time would be a good metaphor for living your life a 'day at a time' so be careful because it is slippery." Then after a brief pause, "And by the way, Howard, if you are not convinced that the ice is thick enough to support you, you will dread every step you take." I saw that application to living my life a day at a time. I was quickly convinced that this might be Divine guidance and that I could trust that this presentation would have Divine support.

I did not mention this experience to anyone else. I believed it and did not want to risk losing the conviction by discussing it with anyone. I had three months to prepare the presentation and I received a great deal of help from some of the best design engineers in the Apache Helicopter program. The presentation was very successful and that experience, coupled with insights I experienced subsequent to that presentation which I was convinced did not originate in my intellect, supported my *growing conviction* of the pervasive Presence and Power of the Spirit of God in my life.

A significant experience connected with this *growing conviction* came out of my reading on pages 351 through 354 of the book "*Pass It On,*" that Bill W. had written the 12 and 12, not to change the Steps but to "deepen and broaden" the experience of the Steps as described in the Big Book for oldtimers and newcomers alike. As I described in Step One of this guide, that led me to come to believe that as stated in the 12 and 12, fully conceding to my innermost self that I was "personally powerless" became bedrock for an unshakeable foundation for life.

As Bill W. promises on page 46 of the Big Book "We found that as soon as we were able to lay aside prejudice and express even a willingness to believe in a Power greater than ourselves we commenced to get results, even though it was impossible for any of us to fully define or comprehend that Power, which is God." . . . "As soon as we admitted the possible existence of a Creative Intelligence, a Spirit of the Universe underlying the totality of things, we began to be possessed of a new sense of power and direction, provided we took other simple steps."

That is exactly what happened to me when I was 13 years sober. In a letter to Father Dowling quoted on page 354 of "*Pass It On*," Bill stated that this "deeper and broader" experience was available to both newcomers and oldtimers alike. It isn't necessary to wait 13 years to see the viability of working each Step in sequence first from the Big Book and then from the 12 and 12, nor in seeing that our personal powerlessness is the bedrock on which we can build happy and productive sober lives. Hopefully, sharing these stories and experiences in working the Steps in that sequence will be helpful to those who read them.

At that time in my sobriety I read on pages 48 and 49 of the Big Book, Bill's description of "The prosaic steel girder is a mass of electrons whirling around each other at incredible speed. These tiny bodies are governed by precise laws, and these laws hold true throughout the material world. Science tells us so. We have no reason to doubt it. . . . the perfectly logical assumption is . . . that underneath the material world and life as we see it, there is an All Powerful, Guiding, Creative Intelligence . . ."

I had read this statement many times during my 13 years of sobriety, and each time I inevitably thought to myself that this is a poor way of describing this process. However, this time when I read it I saw a deeper and broader meaning. Having recently realized the truth of my personal Powerlessness, the words "All Powerful" had a totally different meaning than when I had read it earlier. My concepts of an "All Powerful" God had always been in the context of that Power being totally separate from me. That there was my power and God's "All Power" and the two were separate. Fully conceding to my innermost self that I was personally powerless gave new meaning to the words "All Powerful, Guiding, Creative Intelligence." This description became the basis for seeing that whatever personal power I had had been given to me by this "All Powerful" source of power.

Then, going back to the top of page 49 in the Big Book we read: "Science tells us so. We have no reason to doubt it." What, in general, does Science say about the Spirit and creation? Science tells us that approximately 13.7 billion years ago the universe came into being as an infinitely compressed, infinitely hot, completely undifferentiated state of pure *spirit/energy* located in a region small enough to pull through the eye of a needle. That at some given instant, this tiny universe began to expand, cool and evolve through a seemingly endless series of finely tuned processes and parameters, each process more complex than the previous process, which eventually unfolded into the very improbable life breeding universe that we live in today.

Over my lifetime and yours science has continued its efforts to better understand the creative processes involved in this "Big Bang" creation. Descriptions of some of these slices of time from creation are summarized and shown in the back of this guide as Appendix I, "Science Tells Us So. We Have No Reason to Doubt It." To some of us this information provides a "deeper" meaning of the words "finely tuned processes and parameters." To others, it gives new meaning to Dr. Bob's admonition to "Let's keep it simple."

An important insight for me was that creation began about 13.7 billion years ago with this initial spirit or energy expanding into everything that exists in the universe today and that creation process has continued up to this moment, one moment of creation at a time. I would like to suggest that while it admittedly harbors some distraction to many of us, please read all you can stand to read from appendix I. And then contemplate this fact: The unfolding of the universe took place in wonderful order and harmony for nearly 14 billion years. Then we came into being. What possible sense does it make that we are now responsible for running our lives without help from that same Creative Intelligence.

In addition to Bill's suggestions that we can find additional spiritual strength by looking into science, throughout the first 94 pages of the Big book Bill frequently suggests that we should be open to the value of religious beliefs and practices. Examples of that are presented below:

"They had told of a simple religious idea and a practical program of action." Page 9, Big Book

"It began to look as though religious people were right after all." Page 11, Big Book

"Those having religious affiliations will find here nothing disturbing to their beliefs or ceremonies." Page 28, Big Book

"Not all of us join religious bodies, but most of us favor such memberships." Page 28, Big Book

"Though not a religious person, I have profound respect for the spiritual approach in such cases as yours." Page 43, Big Book

"But later in his room, he asked himself this question: "Is it possible that all the religious people I have known are wrong?" Page 56, Big Book

"Though we have no religious connection, we may still do well to talk with someone ordained by an established religion." Page 74, Big Book

"Be quick to see where religious people are right. . . . " Page 87, Big Book

"We represent no particular faith or denomination. We are dealing only with principles common to most denominations." Pages 93-94, Big Book

Dr. Bob frequently recommended that members read Emmet Fox's essays in the book "*Sermon on the Mount; The Key to Success in Life;*" as well as Henry Drummond's valedictory address to a group of graduating missionaries titled "*The Greatest Thing in the World,*" wherein he used St. Paul's Letter to the Corinthians on love as his text. Most of the foundation principles of Christianity are included in the *Sermon on the Mount.* Among the other essays in Fox's book are those on the Lord's Prayer. One of the best of those is on "Forgive Us Our Trespasses as We Forgive Those who Trespass Against Us." Also, the Book of James in the New Testament was referred to so often in the beginning that some gave serious consideration to naming the fellowship after that book.

As I mentioned previously, soon after Pat and I were married, I basically discarded all my religious beliefs and thereby threw the baby out with the bath water. I made no effort to find any goodness in religion and simply adopted Deism and what I believed were its teachings. In 1985, when I was going through the Second Step first from the Big Book and then from the 12 and 12, I began to see that Bill was largely addressing people like myself who *had thrown the baby out with the bath water.*

In the Second Step essays Bill has us focus on our belligerence, which is essentially the same characteristic that drove us to insist that "we could wrest happiness and satisfaction out of this world if we only managed well." This attitude coupled with alcohol had enabled us to not only feel good but helped many of us achieve a level of material success that we would probably not have reached otherwise. When we finally surrendered so God could smash the obsession that we could someday drink like normal people, we began our recovery from the seemingly hopeless state of mind and body. But many of us retained the conviction that sober, we could manage our lives ourselves.

Then, in the 12 and 12, Bill reminded us that our scientific schooling had taught us that a fundamental principle of scientific method was trial and error; search and research, theory always tested by experiment, never with a closed mind; that "contempt prior to investigation" could only assure us of everlasting ignorance. Then Bill noted that I was the one with the closed mind; that if I was to take an open minded look at AA's success I would realize who was not being scientific? And it wasn't AA, it was me. Then he noted that just a little open mindedness would start the ball rolling, and that once it was rolling Step Two was entering our lives.

He also suggested that perhaps some of us could satisfy our search for faith by making the AA program our higher power. Certainly AA had demonstrated magnitudes more power than I had when it came to stopping drinking and straightening out the wreckage of an alcoholic life. All I had to do was just look around the meeting room; talk to and listen to sober drunks and how the AA program worked for them. At the time, this was the path that made the most sense to me and that I quickly adopted.

Keeping in mind that Bill had encouraged us throughout the Big Book to look for the goodness in religion and to take advantage of what it had to offer. Now, 13 or so years later, when he was writing the 12 and 12, he recognized that thus far many of us had instead focused on negative rather than positive thinking about religion. We had prided ourselves in pointing out the hypocrisy and self-righteousness of some believers, which enabled us to feel superior to them and ignore that this position highlighted our own hypocrisy and self-righteousness.

Next, Bill points out what I believe he was taught by Dr. Harry M. Tiebout in the mid 1940's when Bill was seeking psychiatric help for his depression. That idea was that two related qualities characterized the alcoholic personality: defiant individuality and grandiosity. Therefore, Bill explained, we should not be startled that many of us had taken our turn at defying God. Bill also emphasizes that after we are in AA a while we realize that our defiance had led us to approach God with our demands about what we wanted from Him; seldom asking what he would have us do. Then, ever so gradually, as happened with our obsession to take the first drink, we surrendered our defiance to a level of humility that would allow God to dispel that defiance in favor of our experiencing compliance.

We discovered that with an open-minded look at 'What Science Tells Us," in order to become convinced of the pervasive presence of a creative intelligence, a spirit of the universe underlying the totality of things, manifesting precise law, order and harmony in everything, it gradually became clear that we could not run the show ourselves. By looking for where religious people are right we found that the spiritual principles of humility, open-mindedness, patience, forgiveness, tolerance, kindliness and love are common to most religious denominations and are essential spiritual principles for our recovery from alcoholism.

Very similar to my surrender to being an alcoholic on the streets of San Diego on August 4, 1972, I was at the level of humility where I admitted that I had been completely defeated in my delusion to manage my own life and that I must have the help of a Higher Power to restore me to sanity. Being convinced I turned to Step Three for that help.

Step Three

§

*"Made a decision to turn our will and our lives over
to the care of God, as we understood Him."*

Early in my sobriety it "made sense to me" that if I really
"came to believe in a Higher Power" that could guide me into a
happy comfortable way of life without drinking and using. My
Third Step "Decision" would be based on the strength and sincerity with which I had "Come to Believe." It would be the Second
Step that was difficult; the Third Step would be much easier.

At the start I came to believe that the Program of Alcoholics
Anonymous was the Higher Power that guided me in my life
of sobriety and my first Third Step was to decide to follow the
Program's guidance in ways that "made sense to me." Obviously,
every iteration of working the Steps has brought me closer to,
and strengthens my belief that "A Spirit of the Universe, an All-
Powerful Guiding Creative Intelligence" is my Higher Power
and that my life is now, always has been and always will be in a
partnership with that Spirit.

"This is the how and the why of it. First of all, we had to quit
playing God. It didn't work. Next, we decided that hereafter in

this drama of life; God was going to be our Director. He is the Principal; we are His agents. He is the Father, and we are His children. Most good ideas are simple, and this concept was the keystone of the new and triumphant arch through which we passed to freedom. . . . When we sincerely took such a position, all sorts of remarkable things followed. We had a new Employer. Being all powerful, He provided what we needed, if we kept close to Him and performed His work well. Established on such a footing we became less and less interested in ourselves, our little plans and designs. More and more we became interested in seeing what we could contribute to life. As we felt new power flow in, as we enjoyed peace of mind, as we discovered we could face life successfully, as we became conscious of His presence, we began to lose our fear of today, tomorrow or the hereafter. We were reborn." Pages 62-63, Big Book

One of the most important paragraphs in the Big Book in my search for spirituality starts on the last line of page 48 and continues on at the top of page 49: "The prosaic steel girder is a mass of electrons whirling around each other at incredible speeds. These tiny bodies are governed by precise laws, and these laws hold true throughout the material world." For the first ten years or so every time I read this paragraph I would think that Bill did not do an effective job of describing the behavior of particles in massive bodies. I thought electrons should be described as "whirling around protons and neutrons" rather than "around each other." As my understanding of my personal powerless grew so did my willingness to search for the pervasive presence and power of God in my life. The truth of Bill's statement on page 46 that "As soon as we admitted the possible existence of a Creative Intelligence, a Spirit of the Universe underlying the totality of things, we began to be possessed of a new sense of power and direction . . . " became clearer to me. Then, taking his statement on the top of page 49 out of context so that, ". . . *the perfectly logical assumption is . . . that underneath the material world and life as we see it, there is an All Powerful, Guiding, Creative Intelligence . . .*" I saw the basis for that important leap of faith. If this Spirit underlies the material world then it underlies life as we see it. Not just the physics, chemistry and biology of life, but the circumstances and events of life as well. Chuck C.'s insistence that *nothing* can exist in the universe apart from God; if it exists it must be a part of, seen in that light made sense to me.

"We were now at Step Three. Many of us said to our Maker, as we understood Him: "God, I offer myself to Thee—to build with me and do with me as Thou wilt. Relieve me of the bondage of self, that I may better do Thy will. Take away my difficulties, that victory over them may bear witness to those I would help of Thy Power, The Love, and Thy Way of Life. May I do Thy will always!" We thought well before taking this step making sure we were ready; that we could at last abandon ourselves utterly to Him." (Page 62-3, Big Book)

Now let's turn to Step Three in the 12 and 12 where Bill endeavors to increase the depth and breadth of our understanding of the Steps.

In his essay on Step Three in the 12 and 12, Bill addresses the situation as he saw it at the time. Since the first days of his sobriety he saw himself, and others, come into AA, work the Steps, get sober and stay sober. Like himself, he also saw sober alcoholics working with newcomers to help them get sober and stay sober. However, on page 39 of the 12 and 12 he noted that while these alcoholics had been able to rely on the program to stay sober, that many were still victimized by remorse, guilt, bitterness, envy, hate, financial insecurity and panic, all of which remained from the wreckage of their past. As Bill acknowledged on page 15 of the Big Book, that in his early sobriety he was frequently plagued with "waves of self-pity and resentment" . . . "Many times I have gone to my old hospital in despair. On talking to a man there, I would be amazingly lifted up and set on my feet. It is a design for living that works in rough going." Bill is reported to have continued to fight deep depressions even while he was writing the 12 and 12. (See Page 352, '*Pass It On*') This fact begs the question: "Why is the going so rough for so long after we get sober?"

Throughout his essay on Step Three, and throughout all of his essays on the Steps in the 12 and 12, Bill acknowledged that the level of surrender that resulted from our drinking had been deep enough to allow a Higher Power (God) into our lives to smash the obsession to drink. But in large part selfishness and self-centeredness has remained active in the other areas of our sober lives to block His entry into our lives to help us work the remaining Steps.

Bill uses a locked door as a metaphor for 'self-will' blocking the presence of a Higher Power (God) out of our consciousness and describes the Third Step as the key of willingness that unlocks that door. Later, in the first part of his essay on Step 7 of the 12 and 12, Bill informs us that humility is the basic spiritual principle in each of the Twelve Steps. He states further that the level of humility we experienced in our surrender to our alcoholism in the First Step is the standard we must maintain in order to successfully work the other 11 Steps.

Several years ago when I asked Bob B. to be my sponsor, the first book he asked me to read was titled *"Falling Upward: A Spirituality for the Two Halves of Life,"* by Richard Rohr. This book was very helpful in my finding ways to surrender the first half of my life and "falling upward," into the second half (of course, the halves are not equal chronologically). Since then I have found other observations of Father Rohr to be helpful. As I have noted earlier my Second Step from the Big Book was an intellectual process connected with studies of the ongoing "Big Bang" creation. My Second Step from the 12 and 12 was an opening of my mind to finding goodness in religious practices that made sense to me. In a recent daily meditation Richard Rohr noted that Niles Bohr's Study of Quantum Physics lead him to proclaim that ". . . the universe is not only stranger than we think, but stranger than we can think. . ." to which Father Rohr added that it was also true that "God is not only greater than we think, but greater than we can think." Our answer to finding God cannot be achieved by logical and rational thinking but only through, ". . . love, prayer (Meditation) and conscious participation" with God in the circumstances and events of our lives.

Having intellectually "came to believe," in my Second Step, my Third Step decision to turn my will and my life over to the care of God must include a level of surrender deeper than my intellect to a level of humility where I can, through loving my life, praying and meditating, experience ". . . a personally satisfactory, conscious partnership with the God that made us in the entire business of living." (New *Pair of Glasses*, page 27)

In the next to last paragraph on page 40 of Step Three in the 12 and 12 Bill has italicized essentially the same message he left us on Page 85 of the Big Book: ". . . What we really have is a daily reprieve contingent upon our spiritual condition. Every day is a day when we must carry the vision of God's will into all of our activities. 'How can I best serve Thee—Thy will (not mine) be done.' These are thoughts which must go with us constantly. We can exercise our will power along this line all we wish. It is the proper use of the will."

Those of us who have attended Sandy B.'s annual retreats near Tampa Bay, Florida will recall that near the end of each retreat he would have us set quietly in meditation and he would read to us from Page 36, Step Three in the 12 and 12, where the 'instinct' of the sober alcoholic cries out against having to turn his will and his life over to the care of a Higher Power (God or Anything or Anyone) in fear of becoming nothing more than a doughnut hole. Sandy would then have us imagine that there was a doughnut on the upper left hand part of our table. With our eyes closed we were to pick that doughnut up and imagine that we were looking through that hole, and what we would see . . . and then Sandy would play Louis "Satchmo" Armstrong singing his hit song, "What a Wonderful World."

Step Four

§

"Made a searching and fearless moral inventory of ourselves."

As has been frequently noted the surrender that takes place at a level of humility needed to let God help us is essential for the next succeeding Step to work. To me, that means that I must admit to my inner most self that I am an alcoholic who has to stop drinking but knows he cannot stop without help and asks for help. Then and only then will I have surrendered to a level that I will be able to see that I cannot wrest satisfaction and happiness out of this world by managing my life well; then knowing that I will have to surrender to that but at the same time seeing that I cannot make that surrender without help, then I ask for help. And, fully conceding to our innermost selves that in and of ourselves we are totally powerless becomes solid bedrock on which we can stand while looking at Step Two for help. And so on with each roadblock described in Steps Two and Three which require acknowledging that we have to change and knowing that we cannot change without help, and then asking for help by working the next Step. We will never be Saints because we do not do this perfectly, but our lives get relentlessly better as we continue along this path.

I am including the following story although parts of it fit in subsequent Steps. My experience with the Steps didn't initially follow in direct sequence with the Steps and I jumped around a lot. As I noted earlier I was more or less flying blind under my own guidance after my sponsor Kenny moved to Simi Valley, California. We kept in touch but no longer attended meetings together; and going to meetings with Kenny had been the key to finding solutions to my daily problems at home and at work.

I got off to several false starts in my first attempt at completing a Fourth Step, but I ended up in a spiral notebook writing an autobiography about my resentments, selfishness, dishonesty, fears and sex in chronological sequence in a series of succinct statements. Looking back I see that I got most of the physical and mental abuses I experienced and transmitted when I was a kid (basically before I was in High School) and most of the 'tall poles in the tent' in terms of my behavior that preceded my last few years of drinking. The only important sex issue was that I had been molested by a Protestant school teacher when we moved to Wichita during World War II. The molestation consisted only of touching but afterwards I felt very ashamed and guilty. Those feelings stayed with me through my childhood and into adulthood to the point that I had a great deal of difficulty putting it in my inventory. I decided to put it in my Fourth Step in order to get what benefit that might give me, but I resolved not to mention it in my Fifth Step.

When I was working my way through the Steps again in 1985, I started a Meditation process on the first Three Steps while I was working on my Fourth Step. Basically, I followed the guidance I had received from my mentor and great friend

Frank G., at his home that Saturday morning when he took me through Step 11 in the 12 and 12.

I have included that Guided Meditation on the First Three Steps as APPENDIX II. I am personally convinced that this "conscious" daily practice keeps the neural circuits to these "spiritual beliefs" active in my decision making process as I go through the day.

This format for doing the Fourth Step Inventory in three columns was first shown to me by my second sponsor, George C.; who probably got it from his sponsor Fred E.; and, Fred probably got it from his sponsor, Jack B. At this time, my wife had been going to Al-Anon and had stopped caving in to me every time I insisted on having my way.

When I complained about her unreasonableness to George, he responded by saying "It sounds like we need to go through the Steps again."

"I know," I answered, "But I don't think she has gone through them the first time."

He laughed and said "I mean time for *you* to go through the Steps again."

I could not believe that he thought I was in any way at fault here. Anyway, this is the format he gave me, from the Big Book, to do my Fourth Step.

In retrospect, the words Bill selected for his description on page 62 (in my bold italics) helped once again to emphasize that "self" was the root of my problem. ***"Selfishness—self-centeredness****! That we think is the root of our troubles. Driven by a hundred forms of **fear, self-delusion, self-seeking and self-pity**, we step on the toes of our fellows and they retaliate." . . . "So our troubles, we think, are basically *of our own making*. They arise out of *ourselves*, and the alcoholic is an extreme example of *self-will* run riot, though he usually doesn't think so. Above everything, we alcoholics must be rid of this *selfishness*."

"Being convinced that *self*, manifested in various ways, was what had defeated us, we considered its common manifestations." Page 64, Big Book

Bill W. then started the Big Book inventory guide by pointing out first that: "Resentment is the "number one" offender. " . . . "In dealing with resentments, we set them on paper. We listed people, institutions or principles with whom we were angry." Page 64, Big Book He then gave us detailed instruction on how to complete this part of the Inventory (I have added bold italics to highlight the Big Book's guidance): "We went back through our lives. Nothing counted but thoroughness and honesty." . . . "The first thing apparent was that *this world and its people were often quite wrong*. " . . . "The usual outcome was *that people continued to wrong us and we stayed sore*."

He then suggested a process for reviewing these resentments in order to forgive each and every one of them.

"This was our course: We realized that *the people who wronged us* were perhaps spiritually sick. Though we did not like their symptoms and the way these disturbed us, they, like ourselves, were sick too. We asked God to help us show them the same tolerance, pity, and patience that we would cheerfully grant a sick friend. When a person offended we said to ourselves, 'This is a sick man. How can I be helpful to him? God save me from being angry. Thy will be done.'" . . . "We cannot be helpful to all people, but at least God will show us how to take a kindly and tolerant view of each and every one."

It seems clear to me that Bill has deliberately used the words ***"the people who wronged us"*** to refer to the people, institutions and principles with whom, "we stayed sore."

My personal experience was that when I was "prepared to look at it from an entirely different angle." ... That "they, like ourselves, were sick too. . . "the sick man's prayer" worked for me even though I wasn't conscious of meaning it as a prayer. However, I did consciously read these words for their deeper meanings. Looking at it from an entirely different angle helped me see my part in the resentment. They, like me, wanted their way and in these instances they were in the position of strength so they had their way and I didn't, and I resented them.

After we forgive all the resentments, he wrote: "Referring to our list again. Putting out of our minds t***he wrongs others had done***, (note that these are the words Bill is using to describe resentments) we resolutely looked for our own mistakes. Where had we been selfish, dishonest, self-seeking and frightened?" Here I was taught to now put the resentments out of my mind and complete a three column inventory on each of these defects of character, just like we had done for our resentments. Going back through our lives, "Nothing counted but thoroughness and honesty." Page 67, Big Book

SPECIAL NOTE ABOUT THE FOURTH COLUMN:
In 1977, a couple of AA guys from Arkansas started a series of weekend seminars which were titled "The Big

Book Comes Alive" with Joe and Charlie. These guys transformed A.A.'s understanding of working the Steps from the Big Book, which indeed came alive in the fellowship. Their interpretation of the Big Book's description of the resentment inventory leads to their using a Fourth Column to identify "Our Part" in the resentment. In large part theirs was the first detailed description of the Fourth Step and established the belief that this is the way Bill W. intended it to be done. In discussing the Fourth Column with those who are devoted to that approach it became clear to me that the major value of the Fourth Column is that it is a place for the sponsee and sponsor to identify the mistakes the sponsee made in creating the resentment being addressed; highlighting the sponsee's part; and laying the track for what amends are to be made later. It also seems to me that the best place to use the Fourth Column is when taking the Fifth Step with your sponsor after you have inventoried your resentments, selfish behavior, dishonesty, self-seeking and fears by using the three columns that Bill illustrated for the resentment inventory.

This guide does not use a fourth column in the Fourth Step, but adds it to the Fifth Step. This guide uses the three column inventory format presented on page 65 for all five of the "manifestations of self" listed by Bill in the second full paragraph on page 67: resentments (wrongs others have done) and then where we have been selfish, dishonest, self-seeking and frightened. After going back through our lives 5 times (using a biographical time-line to stay focused) and listed to the best of our ability all the instances we could recall when we had harmed others by these defects of character, we then add a Fourth Column headed (MY PART) as described below to be used by the sponsee and sponsor during the Fifth Step.

It was helpful to me in writing these inventories, to orient myself to the home I was living in and to the relationships I had with the people I lived with, to my neighbors, my friends, my enemies, my employers, employees, and the people institutions and principles that were involved in my life. For me this worked best by identifying my homes. Others might find other bases, such as dates, jobs, etc. more helpful in their lives. The Time-line that fits my inventories of those defects of character is shown below.

TIME FRAME	HOME	LIVED WITH
1932-1941	Milan, Kansas: Apt. behind barber shop	Dad, mom, 2 sisters, 1 brother
1941-1942	Milan, Kansas: 2 story yellow house	Dad, mom, 2 sisters, 1 brother
1943-1945	Wichita, Kansas: Project Housing	Dad, mom, 1 brother
1945-1950	Argonia, Kansas: House by Rail Road	Dad, mom, 1 brother
1950-1953	U.S. Navy	Aboard Ship in Korea
1953-1966	San Diego: Apt and 1st home	Pat, Tim, Mike and Anne
1966-1985	Culver City: Rented & Ranch Road home	Pat, Tim, Mike and Anne
1985-1991	Chandler, AZ: Alamo Drive home	Pat and Anne
1991-1995	Culver City: Ranch Road home	Pat
1995-Present	Gilbert, AZ.: Western Skies Drive home	Pat

NOTE: In providing examples of the content and format of the three column inventory that Bill instructs us to use in our Big Book portion of the Fourth Step, I have included only samples of my actual inventory. The actual inventories include institutions, people and principles from every time period of my life. Additionally, the people and places used for my timeline are simply guides to help me recall all the places, people and institutions included in my actual inventory.

RESENTMENT IS THE NUMBER ONE OFFENDER.
I then organize my first inventory list into three columns:
The first headed: *I'm resentful at*: the second headed: *The cause:* and the third headed: *Affects my*: See Page 65, Big Book.

In doing the Resentment inventory I looked at each person, institution and principle that I could remember having a relationship with (not limited to those listed; they were included but also served a starting points to find others) during each time frame. There were two categories of resentments that I listed: First, when someone forced me to do something I did not want to do; and Second, when I tried to get others to do what I wanted and they resisted. In both categories I was not having my way, and I was trying to "wrest satisfaction and happiness out of this world . . . " by having my way. I listed these people, institutions or principles in the first column by name. Clearly, selfishness and self-centeredness was at the root of these resentments. I was not having my way and it made me angry.

In the second column, under The cause, I succinctly but specifically list the reasons I have the resentment.

Note: In this inventory I did not generalize by stating that my dad beat me. I listed each specific beating that I could remember. This is necessary to ensure that all beatings that are remembered are also forgiven, thereby changing the brain chemistry and pathways. However, I did list some generalizations which were accurate and seemed appropriate to me.

In the third column, under Affects my, I listed what it was about me that was affected (or effected) by this resentment. Examples in the Big Book include: self-esteem, our pocketbooks, our ambitions, our personal relationships (including sex) as well as our emotions: such as fear; anger of course was at the core of each resentment. Page 64-5, Big Book

I'M RESENTFUL AT	THE CAUSE	AFFECTS MY
(1932-41) My Dad	When I was 4 or 5, he was drunk and jerked me out of the shower and beat me. Mom made him stop. He left, came back drunker, and beat me some more. Backside was welts, black and blue from shoulder blades to calves of legs.	Security, fear, self-esteem, hate, pride
	When I was six or seven, I sharpened his straight razors and he whipped me for four days.	Traumatized me with fear; Hate, self-esteem, pride
	When I was 6 or 7, a school teacher slapped me and dad beat me with the starter rope and his belt, spread eagled on my bed.	Security, fear, self-esteem, pride, trust
	Frequent other whippings, spankings and hitting.	Self-esteem, pride, hate
	Ongoing verbal abuse: "You are never going to amount to anything." "You are worthless as tits on a boar hog." Etc.	Self-esteem, pride Security, unworthy

I listed every resentment that I could remember with every relationship I had while living behind the barber shop, including mom, sisters, brother, friends, teachers, other adults, schools, Sunday school, God, Jesus, Satan, etc. in the same detail as the above examples. Then I moved to our next home, re-orienting myself there, and listed all those resentments until I was current. When I went through the Steps again at a later time I would add anything that I remembered that I had not included in earlier inventories, and then I would bring that inventory up to date.

When I had listed all of my resentments I considered each one of them as the Big Book describes in the last two paragraphs on page 66 and the first two paragraphs on page 67: "This was our course: We realized that the people who wronged us were perhaps spiritually sick. Although we did not like their symptoms and the way these people disturbed us, they like ourselves were sick too." I then reorient myself as I do in the Second Step in order to be conscious of God's Presence and Power. I do this every time I am going to Pray to God. Then, "We asked God to help us show (give) them the same tolerance, pity, and patience that we would cheerfully grant a sick friend." . . . "We cannot be helpful to all people, but at least God will show us how to take (give) a kindly and tolerant view of each and every one." At first I did this simply because the Big Book suggested it. Later I did it because it is the only thing that worked for me.

My *first inventory* included most of the "tall poles" in the tent of my little life as far as resentments go. I went over all the resentments that I had listed and I asked God to help me show them the same tolerance, patience, kindness and pity/compassion that I would gladly show a sick friend. This process not only worked to get rid of the resentments but I know now that it started the building of new neural pathways from anger to forgiveness.

Using my dad for an example: My dad joined AA in July of 1946 and except for a one weekend slip in 1947, he stayed sober for the rest of his life, dying of a heart attack at an AA meeting in March, 1951. My first inventory was written in 1973.

When I considered my resentments of my dad I saw that my dad was filled with insecurities (he had 6 kids in 8 years, 2 died in infancy), during the Great Depression; he had a 7th grade education and believed in "spare the rod and spoil the child." No one knew anything about Attention Deficit Disorder and dad would not have understood the word "trauma." Coupled with that I saw that the beatings and verbal abuse no longer existed any place other than in my head. There is no *quid pro quo*, no barter, no "let's make a deal," involved in this process. Tolerance, pity (compassion), patience and kindness are forgiving. I deliberately forgave him for all my resentments, one at a time. After this experience, I have never felt angry at my dad ever again. This process resulted in my feeling that I had also been forgiven for my selfishness with my kids.

Today I know that all my resentments keep pumping the neuro-transmitters to activate my fight or flight center, and therefore, keep the pleasure centers from activating. This listing of and forgiving of resentments, directly addresses the biochemical imbalances that characterize alcoholism and drug addiction. I also know that I have built up neuro-pathways to automatically react with fear and anger every time I felt these resentments. This forgiveness process creates new neuro-pathways: shutting down "anger pathways" and firing up "forgiveness pathways." In the long run, this results in responding with forgiveness of offences in real time and activates our pleasure centers. This process is extended when working Step 10 throughout our recovery.

It is also important to note that this "forgiveness process" did not take place until I read the "Sick Man Prayer" on pages

66 and 67 of the Big Book, not as a prayer, but reading it with my mind open to the deeper meaning of each idea and phrase. Again, for me, that experience demonstrated the requirement for constructive meditation in every new step in spiritual growth. This is also true in the following 'Forgiveness Experience.'

Once again it is too late to make a long story short, but I wrote the above description of the forgiveness process before 2012, when Pat and I were forced to sell our business. I now have more to say about Forgiveness.

In 1987 I was promoted to the position of Manager of the System Engineering Department of the Helicopter Design Division which was basically the level established by the Peter Principle. Almost immediately technology exploded beyond my level of education with fiber optics, composite materials, and micro-processors being shrunk to half size every year. I soon saw I was not going to be able to keep up and I retired from Engineering Management in 1991. I then had an immediate opportunity to work as an Independent Contractor in the Comedy Business. That soon led into an opportunity to buy an interest in a comedy club in Arizona. This business turned out to be a great deal of fun, gave Pat and I time and money to travel and it was also very profitable in terms of our initial investment. To use Bill W.'s term in the Big Book, "the goose hung high" for the next fifteen years. Then, around 2009, another comedy club owner offered us a lot of money for our club and franchise. My partners and I decided not to sell because we believed we could make as much money as the other guy could and we planned to continue our retirement with that income and then leave it to our children when we really and finally retired.

NOTE: I didn't ask for God's guidance on this decision; clearly God wanted us to keep the Club.

Several years later another club owner offered to buy half of our franchised area to compete with us in our market. We decided to turn that offer down. Later, those two club owners partnered and gained control of booking the Class A comedy performers and with the death of my senior partner we were forced to sell our business to this group. This took place in the summer of 2012.

I was angry and anxious with this turn of events and I started through the Twelve Steps for the I don't know how many times. Shortly I had prepared a new inventory which included a long list of resentments for all of the people, institutions and principles that had been involved in our having to sell the business. I went over every resentment and gave the person I resented tolerance, patience, kindness and pity/compassion for having wronged me. However, soon after completing that process, I read an article about the closing of my old club for remodeling and I was resentful again. Then I repeated the forgiveness process and this time I tried to deepen it. However, there would be another article or phone call about the club and I was again filled with resentments.

In August of 2012 my wife Pat had 2 strokes and developed other serious health problems so I was soon glad that I was no longer in business because she needed me as her fulltime caretaker. She has been remarkably successful in her really courageous effort to recover from them.

However, after a year of resentments followed by forgiveness, followed by the same resentments *ad infinitum*, in August of 2013, we went to spend a couple weeks with our oldest son in Seattle. After we settled in I told our son, who would have 4 years of sobriety in September that I wanted to take some time out while I was there to try again to forgive the resentments that I had for having to sell our business.

Tim was (and still is) studying Emit Fox's writings and he suggested that if I was having trouble with forgiveness, reading Emit Fox's essays on the Lord's Prayer would be helpful. I had read Fox when I had first came to the program and he was too religious for me. Tim more or less shifted his "suggestion" to "insistence" that I should read Fox's essays. In fact he handed me the book and I began to read it. Tim was right. Fox's essays on the Lord's Prayer provided me with my best answers to my forgiveness problems.

My recommendation to everyone who is preparing their resentment list is to read Emmet Fox's essays on The Lord's Prayer before you start the process. I am not going to try to cover it all here but I am going to highlight some of the stuff I needed "to freshen my understanding."

First "Our Father" not only establishes my relationship with God as being that of father and child, but establishes Him as a Divine Spirit and as His child I too am a Divine Spirit. And, as Our Father, He is the loving Father of all mankind.

In the essay addressing Our Daily Bread, I read "In short, we have to train ourselves to look to God, Cause, for all that we need, and the channel (business, investments, savings, or whatever) will take care of itself." As I read this it occurred to me that I had not been asking God to help me forgive these resentments. I had cut God out of the loop altogether and I was trying to give them tolerance, patience, kindness and pity/compassion by myself. I need to look to God for all that I need, including the insight and strength of forgiving.

Then, "Forgive Us Our Trespasses, as We Forgive Them That Trespass against Us." And, "Because we are all one with the great Whole of which we are spiritually a part, it follows that we are one with all men. Just because in Him we live and move and have our being, we are, in the absolute sense, all essentially one." . . . "Of course, nothing in all the world is easier than to forgive people who have not hurt us very much. Nothing is easier than to rise above a trifling loss." But for the "great losses and great resentments" I must seek God's help for Forgiveness.

After I had read the Emmet Fox essays, then read them again, taking notes and giving them more thought, I read the paragraph on Page 84 in the Big Book that starts with: "This brought us to Step Ten." Here was another short essay on inventory, this one ending with "Love and tolerance of others is our code." I then returned to pages 66 and 67 and I carefully read through the next three paragraphs again reading, "We ask God to help us show them the same tolerance, pity (compassion) and patience that we would cheerfully grant a sick friend." Reading to the end of the paragraph with the sentence: ". . . But at least God will show us how to take a kindly and tolerant view of each and every one."

I saw that Love, Tolerance and Pity/Compassion were keys for my Forgiveness process. I had studied, prayed and meditated on Drummond's "Greatest Thing in the World" for years so I knew that "Patience and Kindness "are two of the elements that make up Love; and the others were Generosity, Humility,

Courtesy, Unselfishness, Good Temper, Guilelessness, and Sincerity." I had also studied and meditated on what tolerance and compassion are and how they work in my thinking processes.

I began the process by going through my normal meditation and prayer through the first three Steps, which ends with my consciousness settled in the presence of God. In feeling connected, I also knew that Humility was my knowing that of myself I am nothing, the Spirit within me doeth the work. Then I brought the first person on the resentment list into my mind. I immediately realized that if I was God's spiritual child, so was this guy, and God loved him just as he loved me. I then asked God to help me show him the Tolerance for the thing he did that I resented.

Almost immediately, the question came to me, "When you were fighting with him to keep your business would you have put him out of business if you could have?"

I then remembered that we had gotten a lawyer for just that purpose; and, we were told we didn't really have a case. But the answer to the question was "Yes, in a New York minute."

Then the next question that occurred to me was "Then wouldn't you give him the same tolerance for putting you out of business that you would have given yourself if you could have done the same to him?"

That question was followed by the thought, "This deal is already done; the only thing left for you is to get it out of your head."

Then I simply made it alright with myself that he had done what he had done. I simply cut him some slack, or gave him tolerance. In the same light I saw that he, like me, wanted to have his way and save his business and I felt compassion/pity for him.

Then I went through all of the elements of Love and was guided so that I clearly saw how each element was warranted and was needed 'for giving,' which I was then able to do. I followed that same process in resentment after resentment so that I had carefully and honestly, and with God's guidance, let go of all of my resentments with Love, Tolerance and Compassion/Pity.

Another important point that Emmet Fox makes about Forgiveness is: "On no account repeat this act of forgiveness, because you have done it once and for all, and to do it a second time would be tacitly to repudiate your own work." (And God's) "Afterwards, whenever the memory of the offender or the offense happens to come into your mind, bless the delinquent briefly and dismiss the thought. Do this; however many times the thought may come back. After a few days it will return less and less often until you forget it altogether."

Clearly, this spiritual principle addresses the brain chemistry of 'neural plasticity,' which recognizes that if you "fire it you wire it, and if you don't use it you lose it." That is how it has worked for me.

Pat and I recently attended the performance of one of our favorite comics and personal friends at the club. The new owners have truly upgraded the facility with new computers, sound system and architecture. We enjoyed the show and we left honestly hoping the best for them.

A final note: I started the actual process at noon and by the time I had gone through all of my resentments, with every person, institution and principle, it was after dark. So, it only took me one year, one long afternoon and one evening to get it done and get it over with.

There is no doubt in my mind and my experience of this process that it transforms my brain chemistry and creates new neural pathways from anger to forgiveness.

BEING SELFISH IS THE NUMBER TWO OFFENDER.
Please note once more that Bill, in his description of preparing our Resentment or Grudge List, wrote, "The first thing apparent was that this world and its *people were often quite wrong.* To conclude that *others were wrong* was as far as most of us ever got. The usual outcome was that *people continued to wrong us and we stayed sore.*" Then, "We began to see that the world and its people really dominated us. . . . the *wrong doing of others,* fancied or real, had power to actually kill." (My italics, not Bill's) This language tells me that resentments are the "wrongs others have done." Therefore, when Bill writes "Putting out of our minds the wrongs others had done," I think he means that because we have forgiven them we are no longer addressing resentments or the *wrong doing of others, fancied or real,*" so "...we resolutely looked for our own mistakes. Where had we been selfish, dishonest, self-seeking and frightened".... in our lifetime history of relationships with people, institutions, and principles.

I organized my second inventory which was on ***my being selfish*** into three columns. The first column is headed: ***I was*** *selfish with*; the second column is headed: ***In what way***: and the third column with: ***Affects my***:

Being victims of the insane delusion that our satisfaction and happiness depends on our managing our lives well, we assert our self-will into the lives of others in order to have our way. When we didn't have our way we held resentments. As noted on page 61 of the Big Book, "He may be kind, considerate, patient, generous; even self-sacrificing. On the other hand, he may be mean, egotistical, selfish and dishonest." Whichever way I behaved, I was selfishly trying to have my way. Now we look at those instances where people caved in to our 'selfishness' because we are their parent, their boss, an authority over them; or they just don't want to go through our angry response if they resist giving us our way.

Orienting ourselves in the same way we did with our resentment inventory, (from home to home), we go back through our lives and relationships and list every person, institution and principle with whom we selfishly imposed our will.

The examples shown below were taken from my inventory during my early sobriety in Culver City, from 1966 t0 1985. My resentment list for Pat during that period was that I resented Pat because she would not go to Fresno with me (Although she had gone the year before); and, she had found out that she did not have to cave in to me and she simply offered to love me through the pain if I was hurt by her refusals. My selfish list, comprised of the people I caved-in to my will, turned out to be much longer than my resentment list, including many more people such as my children, my employees, and essentially everyone I had some position of authority over.

I WAS SELFISH WITH	IN WHAT WAY	AFFECTS MY
1966-1985 Pat	She caved in and went from L.A.: to San Diego, to Oxnard, to Santa Barbara, to Fresno, to Bakersfield and to Palmdale to hear me speak.	Pride, Anger, Envy, Self-esteem, Regret and Unworthiness
Tim	Had to stop playing his drums when I got home.	Anger, Self-esteem and Unworthiness
Tim and Mike	Had to stop playing their music when I got home.	Anger, Self-esteem and Unworthiness
Family	We watched my TV shows, my remote, my movies, my events, my teams, my, my, my.	Authority, Pride, Regret Guilt, Remorse, and Unworthiness.

My sponsor had insisted that I should go through the Steps when I complained that Al-Anon had made Pat unreasonable; that she would no longer listen to my reasons. Until I completed and reviewed this part of my second inventory I had not clearly seen that "selfishness, self-centeredness" was indeed the root of my problem." I did not have and never had had a relationship with any person, institution or principle where I was in it to give; but in every instance I was basically a taker, even though I may have loved them deeply and was trying to be kind.

When I saw this I saw it 'within my inner-most self;' and I did not want to be that way. From this inventory on selfishness I could see that even when I had my way I did not find satisfaction and happiness. It was in preparing this list that I began to see the wisdom of Chuck C's saying we should make our life a 12 step call. We should be of service for fun and for free to help God help His kids. Later I saw that when I was being of service to do the best job I could, first within the program, then to help my family, then my boss, my company, and in all my affairs, I had an ongoing sense of satisfaction and happiness. When I focused on having my way or making money I lost that sense of well-being. As Chuck used to say: "I made my life a 12 Step call, doing for others as he would have me do; for fun and for free. And it made me rich. . . .He, He, Hee, Hee."

DISHONESTY IS THE NUMBER THREE OFFENDER.

Referring to our list again we resolutely look for where we have been dishonest. In the same way as in preparing our resentment inventory we go back through our lives, orienting ourselves from home to home. Dishonesty includes lying, cheating, stealing, telling the truth in such a way as to deceive the other person, denial, etc. etc. etc.. Nothing counts but thoroughness and honesty.

I WAS DISHONEST WITH	IN WHAT WAY	AFFECTS MY
1966-1985 My Employer	I stole test equipment from the Test Lab.	Fear, Guilt, Greed
My boss	I lied to him about drinking, missing work, finishing assignments, being drunk in the store room.	Fear, Self-esteem, Guilt, & Greed
My wife	I lied to her about car brakes not working when I was driving drunk & wrecked car.	Fear, Self-esteem, Pride & Guilt.
My wife	I did not tell her I owed B of A & Credit Union $2,500; nor that I had stolen test equipment.	Fear, Self-esteem, Pride & Envy

This inventory list (as did the others) gave me a mirror in which I could see myself and re-experience the feelings of fear, guilt, remorse and low self-esteem. Most of the 'Effects my:'

feelings keep the fight or flight centers active, never letting me feel pleasure.

In the Third Step I committed myself to living a spiritual life, a life in harmony with my belief about God's Will for me; Dishonesty is not only a manifestation of self-will, it is completely out of sync with God's Will and with reality. Something else that occurred to me when I reviewed my inventory on dishonesty was seeing that when the selfish and self-centered life did not work I would lie, cheat and steal in an effort to make it work or at least to make it look like it worked. Such a life could never be a success.

Self-seeking is the number four offender

Referring to our list again. Putting out of our minds the wrongs other had done we resolutely looked for our own mistakes. Where had we been selfish, dishonest, *self-seeking* and frightened?

Being victims of the insane delusion that our satisfaction and happiness was contingent on our managing our lives well, we assert ourselves to secure a position of authority over others to be in a position that we could control them. Orienting ourselves in the same way we did with our resentment inventory, we go back through our lives and list every person, institution, and principle over which we had sought authority so that we could have our way. Of course, I let myself believe that I was only interested in making more money but in this inventory I discovered I really wanted authority so I could have my way. My baby elephant belief system taught me to believe that the husband and the father were the authority over the house hold; that came with the territory.

I WAS SELF SEEKING WITH	IN WHAT WAY	AFFECTS MY
1966-1985 My wife	I took the position that the husband was the authority over the house hold.	Unworthy, pride, And remorseful
	When Pat joined Al-Anon I validated her joining but told her that Bill W. had had Lois start Alanon to keep them out of AA.	Authority pride, remorse, unworthy and dishonest
	When Pat joined OA I validated her but said if there were as many drunken people in AA as there are fat people in OA I wouldn't go to AA.	Authority, pride remorse and guilt
	I said her minister took 45 minutes to make the point that Chuck C. made in 5 minutes, when Chuck didn't make the point at all.	Authority, remorse and Guilt.
	In my actual self-seeking inventory there were 28 instances of this self-seeking behavior over Pat while living in this home.	
My community	My boys and I were precinct captains to elect City Councilmen so I could be appointed City Commissioner for special police protection.	Unworthy, pride, and dishonest
My kids	I was the authority over everything: their music, games, TV, books, and haircuts	Unworthy, pride, fear and remorse.
My employees	I was the boss. Do it my way or be insubordinate and lose your job.	Pride, Envy, and Greed Fear and guilt/remorse

A careful review of this self-seeking inventory revealed that I was obsessed with my being seen as the authority in every area of my life. Although I subordinated myself to higher authorities in my life I couldn't say that Pat's Minister was a better speaker than Chuck C. because whatever I was doing had to be better than what any of my 'subordinates' were doing. The same was true with AA and Alanon, AA and OA, and in all of my affairs. Also, I had been unaware of my being like that until I did this inventory.

Fear is the number five offender

Referring to our list again we resolutely looked at our fears. We put them on paper just the way we did our resentments, selfishness, dishonesty and self-seeking. Once again going back through our lives, from home to home (or period to period) listing our fears. FEAR! "This short word somehow touches about every aspect of our lives. It was an evil and corroding thread; the fabric of our existence was shot through with it." (Page 67, Big Book) We now know that we are 'spring-loaded' to fear and anger by our brain chemistry.

I WAS AFAID OF	IN WHAT WAY	AFFECTS MY
1932-1941 My dad	On the last day of school in the first grade I nearly threw myself under the rear wheels of a gas truck because I was afraid I had failed the first grade and did not want to face him with my report card. I had not failed.	Pride, Envy, Guilt and security.
	After my first beating I was always afraid of him whipping me or abusing me verbally, which he frequently did.	Pride, Guilt, security and self-esteem.
1950-1953 Not getting job	Afraid I would not get a job as an electrician when I was discharged from the Navy. Pat's dad helped me get an Apprentice Tool Maker's job at Boeing Wichita.	security, self-esteem and Pride
1956-1966 Lay-off	In 1959 I was immobilized with fear that I I would be laid off as a toolmaker from Ryan. I was laid off on Friday and hired at GD/A Monday as an entry level Engineer.	Self-esteem, guilt, Pride and security
1966-1985 Work	From 1973 through 1976 I was afraid Hughes would lose Apache contract to Bell. We won.	Security, Pride, and self-esteem.

The Big Book was right in my case. Fear touched almost every aspect of my life. Knowing now what we do about the abundance of neuro transmitters activating our fight or flight centers this should be no surprise. After we have listed all of our fears, the Big Book says, on page 68: "We reviewed our fears thoroughly. . . . We asked ourselves why we had them. Wasn't it because self-reliance failed us? Self-reliance was good as far as it went, but it didn't go far enough. . . . Perhaps there is a better way. . . . We think so. For we are now on a different basis; the basis of trusting and relying upon God."

In 1981, I had gradually begun to open my mind to the possible existence of God actually participating in my life. Sometime in 1982 or 83, I saw that I needed to work all the Steps again, including God in all of them, but especially to include God in the Steps as they were described in the Big Book. I was indeed trying to learn to trust in God, so the idea of being on a basis of trusting and relying upon God was very meaningful to me for the first time. "We are in the world to play the role He assigns. Just to the extent that we do as we think He would have us, and humble rely on Him, does He enable us to match calamity with serenity." It was a long list, but I went over every fear I had listed and reviewed it carefully.

I was probably an Attention Deficit Disorder kid and I got in trouble all the time. I was afraid I would get in trouble and I frequently did. I was very afraid of my dad and he was abusive to me very early in my life and that certainly put the fear of dad in me; (Also, a fear of all the authorities in my life). Looking at each fear I had listed I determined that most of the results I had feared didn't actually happen. In this way I saw that if I had participated just the way I had (self-reliance works as far as it goes) and then had trusted Divine Order to produce the right outcome I would have pretty much had a fear-less life.

I also found that most of the results I feared that had actually happened turned out to be the best things that could have happened for me. For example: I was an electrician in the Navy and had learned to be a good practical electrician, in particular I had learned trouble shooting logic, good maintenance design practices (no 'in the way' removals, etc.) and that 17 to 20 year old high school graduates without much maintenance experience were going to have to keep the weapons working on the battle field. This was very important information for an Apache Helicopter Designer to know. I would have gotten nowhere as a civilian electrician. In addition, as a toolmaker I learned Engineering tolerance requirements, manufacturing processes, and engineering design relationship to production methods. GD/A had sent me to a Graduate Course in Engineering Statistics at UCLA when I worked for them in San Diego. All of that practical experience coupled with limited specialized technical engineering training was very valuable information for a Helicopter Design Engineer.

My fears of not getting to be a civilian electrician and getting laid off as a tool maker did in fact happen. But, in 1985, when I reviewed my fears I saw that I had, in essence, gained a Master's Degree in Practical Engineering knowledge working as an Electrician's Mate in the Navy and as a Tool Maker at Boeing Wichita and Ryan in San Diego.

If I had had my way I would have never been in Engineering Design but would have been an electrician or tool maker. In these instances I could see that while I experienced "*...an evil and corroding thread* ... through the fabric of my existence." God had in fact been pulling *a Golden Thread through every circumstance and event in my life* that I had never experienced because of my ongoing fight/flight center being overactive biochemically. Seeing that I could have successfully trusted God's outcome better than the one I wanted has helped me be less afraid of fearful outcomes. However, I am not going to have my selfish way because "selfishness and self-centeredness" can never really work for me or anyone else. Mr. Howard Hughes is an excellent example of that; he didn't appear to be a happy and satisfied man, although he was a super individual achiever. I am convinced "...that any life run on self-will can hardly be a success." This 'knowledge' shuts down neural transmitters that keep the "fight or flight" center over active and the pleasure centers can kick in and gives me peace of mind.

Now, having finished each of the three column inventories, I suggest you add a Fourth Column to each inventory: Resentments, Selfish, Dishonesty, Self-seeking and Fear and head that column with the words MY PART.

Now about the number six offender: Selfish and harmful sex.

Neither the Big Book nor the 12 and 12 say this but I believe this next inventory should cover all of the things we get 'addicted" to for short term pleasures that do not address our long term pain. This inventory should include not only harmful and selfish sex behavior, but porn, compulsive overeating, compulsive gambling, all mind altering chemicals, etc.

As we have done before, we can go back through our lives, from home to home, or whatever breakdown works best for you, but now, rather than listing the behavior in columns, in each instance, answer the questions in the first full paragraph on Page 69 of the Big Book, getting it all down on paper and take a look at it:

In regard to sex (and other short term pleasures we get addicted to) Where had we been selfish? Where had we been dishonest? Where had we been inconsiderate? Whom had we hurt? Did we unjustifiable arouse jealousy, suspicion or bitterness? Where were we at fault? What should we have done instead? Remember, "Nothing counts but thoroughness and honesty." Again, go back through your "time-line" and answer those 7 questions on every appropriate sexual relationship.

In answer to the question, what should we have done instead? In my own life I have discovered that I cannot let my mind entertain the idea of me caving in to any short term pleasure or I will become obsessed with it even though I do not act on it. Just entertaining ideas results in unnecessary struggles and in becoming dissatisfied with the present situation. *"If we wire it, we fire it and if we don't use it we lose it."* What works best is to immediately dismiss the idea of any such options, just like we do with drinking or drugging.

After I had completed my Fourth Step Inventory as it is described in the Big Book I carefully read Bill's Essay on the Fourth Step in the 12 and 12, keeping in mind that these essays do not describe a different Fourth Step process but broaden and deepen the Fourth Step described in the Big Book.

Early in his 12 and 12 essay on the Fourth Step Bill notes that our desires for sex relations, for companionship, and for emotional and material security are God given and good. But he adds, that for many of us these desires cross over a line and become demands; demands for far more of these things than are needed for our own good and for the good of others. These desires became obsessions of the mind; children of the ego, and continued to give us problems long after our active alcoholism had receded.

Next, Bill turns to the preparation of a list of these obsessions of the mind. In order to avoid confusion over just what he is talking about he decided to focus on a recognized list of violations of moral principles: the seven deadly sins of pride, greed, lust, anger, gluttony, envy, and sloth. As a gentle reminder to myself I looked each of these up in my Webster's.

Pride:	Inordinate self-esteem, conceit. A delight or elation arising from some act or possession. Proud or disdainful behavior or treatment. An ostentatious display.
Greed:	Inordinate or reprehensible desire of acquiring and possessing. Avarice.
Anger:	A strong feeling of displeasure and of antagonism.
Lust:	To have an intense desire or need; usually sexual desire. Lasciviousness.
Gluttony:	Excess in eating or drinking.

Envy: A painful or resentful awareness of an advan-
        tage enjoyed by another joined with a desire to
        possess the same advantage.
Sloth: Disinclination to action or labor; indolence;
        see Lazy.

Now Bill describes Step Four as the start of a lifetime practice, and on page 52 of the 12 and 12, suggests that many of us were only able to make a rough order of magnitude review of our conduct up to now, and thereby exposed only the most obvious and troublesome personal flaws in our Big Book Fourth Step. He suggests that our own best judgment should be used in answering certain remaining questions about ourselves. Then Bill lists approximately 30 questions starting with the last paragraph on page 50 on through page 52 of the 12 and 12. The first question being, "When and how . . . " and goes on to ask how our selfish sex relations hurt others and ourselves.

In continuing our "lifetime" process of self-examination, I wrote each question down on paper and then answered it as thoughtfully and thoroughly as I could, keeping the seven deadly sins in mind as I answered each question.

Step Five

§

"Admitted to God, to ourselves, and to another
human being the exact nature of our wrongs."

"HAVING MADE OUR PERSONAL INVENTORY, what shall we do about it? We have been trying to get a new attitude, a new relationship with our Creator, and to discover the obstacles in our path. We have admitted certain defects: we have ascertained in a rough way what the trouble is; we have put our finger on the weak items in our personal inventory. Now these are about to be cast out. This requires action on our part, which, when completed, will mean that we have admitted to God, to ourselves, and to another human being, the exact nature of our defect." Page 72, Big Book

Many AA members since 1977, when Joe and Charlie began their "Big book Comes Alive Seminars" have found it valuable (even essential) to add a Fourth Column to their Inventories to record "MY PART" in the problem being addressed and focused on what amends and what changes in behavior are needed to fully address the problem. In my opinion, that Fourth Column is more effective if it is completed as part of the Fifth

Step which is a scheduled meeting between the sponsor and the sponsee for the purpose of reviewing the sponsee's inventory. Then, when going through the inventory with their sponsor, the sponsor can be of major assistance in helping the sponsee identify the sponsee's part in each problem. These insights will be of special value when the sponsee is working the Sixth, Seventh, Eighth and Ninth Steps.

Again, my first time through the Steps I did not follow the exact sequence of the Steps. But since this guide is based in large part on my experience with the Steps I have decided to tell the story the way it happened. Therefore, before we actually go into my experience with the Fifth Step I will briefly describe how I got there.

When I was brand new the thought of making a list of my character defects and then discussing them with another person was simply not going to be something I would ever do. That was the major reason that I was not going to work the Steps at all. I had convinced myself that I could correct my behavior by not drinking and going to meetings, and then maintain that good character a day at a time. In my first few weeks I described that theory to Kenny and he had no apparent objections to it. He insisted that I should go to meetings and listen for stuff that was shared, don't drink between meetings and after I started helping Frank with the Setup of our Home Group meetings he announced he was moving to Simi Valley.

After Kenny moved to Simi Valley I drove out to see him at least once a week. I remember telling him what Don G. had said about working the Steps and he acknowledged his understanding but didn't really encourage me to start the Steps.

One evening Kenny called me and said that he was coming to Culver City the next morning and would like to have lunch with me. I told him I was working the Steps but we did not discuss any of that in detail. At lunch the next day, he told me that sometimes newcomers had problems that needed to be addressed before they could actually finish the Steps and then asked me if I had anything like that in my life. I told him about stealing the test equipment, and that it was calibrated so that when the test lab called it in for recalibration it would be discovered missing, and then some hell would break loose. I told him that the "fence" I gave it to ran off and that I had no idea where the equipment was. I added that when I was drunk I had told the bartender in the Tattle Tale that if anyone was looking to buy some test equipment I could get it for them. So, if Security went to the local watering holes asking about test equipment the chances were my name would come up.

Kenny had a worried look on his face, which was not reassuring to me, and he asked me who the fence was. I told him his first name and that he used to drink at the Tattle Tale but had disappeared. Kenny told me that he would see if he could help me and would call me back that afternoon. Within two hours he called me at work and he told me where the equipment was, how much it would cost me to get it back, and that I had better get it back today because the people that had it didn't want it around if security might be looking for it.

I called Pat and told her I was coming home early and I needed to talk to her. I went home and told her about stealing the equipment and needing to get it back today so that I could return it. Several weeks earlier I had gotten paid for a side job I had gotten in San Diego and I had used that money to pay the debts I had that Pat had not known about. She had not been happy about that. Now we were going to have to go to the bank and borrow money to pay for equipment I had stolen. But she was more surprised and frightened than she was angry and we went to the bank and borrowed the money.

Pat set in the car when I went into the business place to get the test equipment back. The owner of the business and I hardly looked at each other. I gave him the money and he gave me the equipment, which was packaged in a suitcase, and I took it out and put it in the trunk of my car. I drove Pat home and we set in the driveway for a moment.

"Pat, I am terribly sorry about this. Please forgive me." I told her.

"Is there anything else like this coming up in the future?" she asked.

"No, nothing like this." I answered, thinking about stuff I had included in my Fourth Step, but knowing there was nothing else like this.

"Okay, then," she said, "You are forgiven."

Pat went into the house and I drove back to work with the equipment. I had no trouble getting the equipment back into the plant through the guard gate. The guard knew me and hardly looked up. I took the equipment up to Tom's office and told him, "Tom, I had stolen this and I am bringing it back."

Tom looked surprised for just a second and then said, "Don't bring it to me, take it to the calibration lab, that's where it belongs."

"I know that much Tom, but I am required to make direct amends."

"Just take it down to the calibration lab and turn it in. And don't say anything to them about where it has been." He told me as he looked at the clock, and added, "Then go home and I'll see you in the morning."

I took the equipment to the calibration lab, checked it in for recalibration, and that was the last time I saw it. I went home and had dinner but I did not go to a meeting. Pat asked me what happened at work and I told her. She asked if I was in trouble with Tom. I told her I didn't think so, but I would know for sure tomorrow. We went to bed early and I actually slept fairly well.

I had set the alarm to wake up and go in early. When I got to my office Tom had left a note on my desk to come to his office when I got to work. On my way to his office I realized for the first time that I might be in serious trouble with him. When I went in to see him he smiled and poured us both coffee and we set down at his desk.

"Howard, I want to talk about that equipment you brought in yesterday. I had it expedited through calibration and it is in perfect working order. What I want to tell you is that while I don't know where the equipment has actually been, I do know that it was not stolen. How I know that is that the company has the equipment. If it had really been stolen we wouldn't have it, would we?"

"No, I guess not." I answered, feeling a deep sense of relief.

"Now, I also want to tell you not to tell anyone else about this. Company policy is that if someone steals anything from the company we have to fire them. There are no provisions for bringing the equipment back." He said with a smile. "So keep this between us."

I assured him that I wouldn't tell anyone else about it, and I tried to thank him for giving me a break. He just waved me off.

The next morning, when I first started waking up I gradually realized that the test equipment problem was over. A good feeling started coming up my body as I sat on the edge of the bed, leaving goose bumps on the back of my hands and neck. It was the same feeling I had had when I took my first drink. Also, like when I had my first drink, that good feeling was transforming my life. Somehow, I have never felt the same about life since I took the equipment back.

Tom and I didn't mention it again until months later when I again tried to thank him. He turned the table on me to explain how much more he trusted me from my bringing the equipment in.

I was very slow to put this together but this experience highlights a very important fact about our gradual recovery. When we drink alcohol or take sedative drugs to lower our anxiety level, it always results in our ending up feeling more anxious than we were before we started. When I was freed from anxiety through working the steps (taking the equipment back for example) I may indeed experience a short term elevated pleasure that doesn't last very long, but I never drop down lower than I started.

Let's say that on a scale of 0 to 10, with 0 being the worst that I can feel and 10 being the best I can feel, during the last days of my drinking I would start my day at about a 3.0. When I took my first couple of drinks I would go to an 8.0, but would soon be sick and puking my guts out. When I woke up from that I would have dropped down to say 2.5, gradually moving back to a 3.0. When I took the equipment back I was running about 4.5 on the average day; when I woke up after taking the equipment back I was feeling an 8.0. When the 8.0 wore off as a result of just living the day, my feeling dropped to maybe 4.6, but it didn't go lower than I had felt when I started the short term pleasure.

When we are drinking our lives get worse never better. When we are working the program our lives get better never worse.

As it turned out, my sponsor Kenny S. had been a High School chum of Kenny F., the fence that had taken the equipment. They had also shared an apartment when they were both between wives and they were drinking together. Kenny S joined AA and Kenny F. had gotten a part time job fencing stolen test equipment. After our talk, Kenny, my sponsor, had called Kenny F. about the equipment explaining to him that the guy that had stolen it had to have it back, that Company Security would be involved before long and after that maybe the FBI. Kenny F. told my sponsor Kenny where the equipment was and what it would cost me to get it. My sponsor then went to the machine shop that had the test equipment, told them the authorities would be involved if I didn't get it back. They were immediately willing to cooperate and within two hours of our meeting he called me and told me where and how I could get the test equipment back.

Later in my sobriety, when I was invited to speak at meetings, I told the story about taking the equipment back and getting the 'high' feelings the next morning. One evening after my talk, a guy came up, showing me his identification and identifying himself as having been the FBI agent that would have investigated that missing equipment. He too was now a sober member of Alcoholics Anonymous, very active in the Police Officers AA Programs. Later he invited me to lead a 'Police Officer's AA Retreat" at Big Bear Mountain that was attended by police officers from five counties in Southern California.

I would frequently hear people at meetings describe how God had done one thing or another for them to solve difficult problems they could not have solved without His help. I was generally understanding about such fantasies but I was completely oblivious to the coincidences in my life being anything except coincidences.

Soon after I had taken the test equipment back and Tom had let me off the hook I finished my first Fourth Step. I then ran in to George C. at a meeting. As usual, following his friendly greeting he asked me "How is your Fourth Step coming along, Howard?"

"I got it finished George," I told him.

The next time I saw George he asked me "How did your Fifth Step go?"

"I have not done my Fifth Step yet," I responded, once again feeling like George was starting to get under my skin.

"That's the Step that really changes our lives Howard. You want to hurry and get that one done." That took place at the Tuesday night Beginner's Meeting at my Home Group.

Then I saw George at the "Easy Does It" group meeting the next night. I cringed when I saw his big smile and I felt like he was coming over to harass me. "Did you do that big Fifth Step yet?" he asked me.

"No, George," I told him, "I haven't done it yet. But if you come over to my house Saturday I will do my Fifth Step with you." I was surprised to hear myself say that; I had not intended to say it. I just heard myself say it.

"What time do you want me to be there?" George responded.

"How about 1:00 in the afternoon?" I answered.

"I'll be there." George told me, we shook hands and he walked away smiling for ear to ear.

George was on time the next Saturday at 1:00 pm. Pat and I and the kids had lunch at 12:00, Pat did the dishes and they left for Whittier, Nixon's birthplace, to spend the afternoon with Pat's Aunt Lou. She told me she would call to make sure we were finished before she came home.

I had made a pot of coffee and expected to make more. George and I sat down in the den with our coffee and my spiral notebook. I was more than a little nervous and I asked, "How do you want to get started with this George?"

George smiled, thought for a second, looked straight at me, and said "Why don't we start by your telling me the stuff you had decided not to tell me at all. That way we will get the hard stuff out of the way and the rest will be easy. By your telling me everything the Fifth Step will really work. If you withhold stuff it doesn't work nearly as well and, it may not work at all."

I started out with the molestation experience and George just kept the same look on his face. George was an actor, a very handsome guy with white hair; although other people in that business didn't think he was very good, he was good enough to act interested without acting shocked. He turned out to be the right guy to listen to my Fifth Step. We went right through it. I added details when I felt the need to and he stayed awake and acted interested, but not too interested. I thought I had put a lot of information in that Step. I believe it was more than 45 pages of succinct notes.

Pat called at six and I told her I only had a few pages left and that I would call her.

When I finished I said "Well that's it, George." What do you think?"

"Well", he smiled, "I think you did a really great job for a first Fourth and Fifth Step. My sponsor, Fred, told me that we would probably need to take another inventory down the road, but I think this was great."

"Do you have any suggestion for me about any of this?" I was surprised that I asked that because I was happy with his comment and I was really ready to stop.

"Just a couple of things that Fred told me about my Fourth and Fifth Step that seem to apply to yours. First, about the Fears you listed, look that list over and see how many of the things you were afraid would happen that didn't actually happen. I was surprised and helped a great deal by doing that. " Pausing for a moment he added, "About the molestation, Fred told me that kids are victims in those situations, but if as adults we hold on to shame and guilt we are volunteers. Don't hang on to the guilt and fear, you were a victim and the other guy was sick. We ask God to help us forgive the sick people in our lives who hurt us. Okay Howard, do you have anything else?"

"Yes I do George. My sponsor, Kenny, moved to Simi Valley, and I need someone local as a sponsor. Would you please be my sponsor?"

"Of course I will, Howard. I am honored that you asked me." He paused for a moment and added "We will just continue on from here and we will talk from time to time about how you are doing. On the other hand, if you want to do this now, I suggest you might read the last paragraph on page 75 of the Big Book, just follow those directions carefully and as it says on page 76, when you feel ready, pray that Seventh Step prayer." He paused for another second and told me, "I'll get out of here now and let you and your family get back together."

I called Pat and told her we were through and that George had left. She said that they were tired and would start right home.

I actually read the bottom two paragraphs on page 75 of the Big Book. The second paragraph on Page 75 describes a series of feelings you might have after you have finished the Fifth Step. I sat quietly after I read the prayer and was aware that I felt relief of some kind and thought that might be the beginning of "a spiritual experience" mentioned in that paragraph. I know I did feel ". . . that the drink problem has disappeared," but that had happened sometime earlier; although that feeling was deeper than ever after completing my Fifth Step with George. Then it says: "We feel we are on the Broad Highway, walking hand in hand with the Spirit of the Universe." I was sure that that feeling hadn't happened for me.

In the third part of the First Step, our admissions of our personal powerlessness led to a growing awareness that whatever power and knowledge we do have had been given to us by some other source of Power. We have never generated any of the power ourselves; in and of ourselves "we are personally powerless." Practicing meditation (awareness), self-examination and prayer has enhanced our awareness of the presence and power of God's Spirit underlying the totality of things, and has helped us establish a more direct personal relationship with this Spirit.

Now we once again become conscious of the presence of the Spirit of the Universe, and we admit every defect of character that we have listed in our inventory through our consciousness to our Higher Power; and in way of self-examination we become open to seeing a deeper meaning of how each instance relates to some defect of character (neuropathway) we have developed in our behavior. In that way we can admit to God, and then thinking each defect through, to ourselves.

In practicing this, I discovered that I have been to some extent selfish and self-centered in every relationship in my life and that I had not known that about myself but I had thought that I was, in large part, an unselfish giver. Just how we "Admitted to God and to ourselves. . ." is not described in much detail in the Big Book or the Twelve and Twelve, but my experience in repeatedly going through the Steps has been that my insight into my selfish character through a series of thorough and honest inventories has resulted in my seeing that selfishness is indeed the root of my trouble.

As stated above, "This requires action . . . which, when completed, will mean that we have admitted to God, to ourselves, *and to another human being,* the exact nature of our defects." . . . This is perhaps difficult---especially discussing our defects with another person. We think we have done well enough in admitting those things to ourselves. There is doubt about that. In actual practice, we usually find a solitary self-appraisal insufficient. Many of us thought it necessary to go much further. We will be more reconciled to discussing ourselves with another person when we see good reasons why we should do so. The best reason first: If we skip this vital step, we may not overcome drinking." . . . ". . . they had not learned enough of humility, fearlessness and honesty, in the sense we have found it necessary, until they had told someone else *all* their life story." Page 72-73, Big Book

In the August 1961 Grapevine article titled "Honesty," Bill W. described how his New England family had taught him the importance of keeping all of his business commitments and contracts. Later in life he allowed his respected business honesty to become a cover under which he could hide the many serious defects that manifested in the other parts of his life. That was also my experience, especially when I was in Engineering Management at Hughes. At Hughes we were directed to always respond as honestly as we could in answering all of our customer's questions. I would brag to Pat about my company's integrity---and my own--- while I lied, cheated and stole in the other areas of my alcoholic life.

"When we decide who is to hear our story, we waste no time. We have a written inventory and we are prepared for a long talk." . . . "We must be entirely honest with somebody if we expect to live long or happily in this world. Rightly and naturally, we think well before we choose the person or persons with whom to take this intimate and confidential step." . . . "We pocket our pride and go to it, illuminating every twist of character, every dark cranny of the past. Once we have taken this step, withholding nothing, we are delighted. We can look the world in the eye. We can be alone at perfect peace and ease. Our fears fall from us. We begin to feel the nearness of our Creator. We may have had certain spiritual beliefs, but now we begin to have a spiritual experience. The feeling that the drink problem has disappeared will often come strongly. We feel we are on the Broad Highway, walking hand and hand with the Spirit of the Universe." Page 75, Big Book

On Page 55 of the 12 and 12 Bill W. points out that all of the Twelve Steps are constructed to deflate our egos, and in that regard, few Steps are harder than Step Five. Emphasizing that if we have seen the depth and width of all of the experiences we had previously tried not to remember and how deeply we had hurt ourselves and others, then we can affirm the need to share that tormenting behavior with another human being.

Many of us would declare that without a fearless admission of our defects to another human being we could not stay sober. It seems plain that the grace of God will not enter to expel our destructive obsessions until we clearly see that our past behavior stands between us and the sunlight of the Spirit; that unaided there is little we can do to change that behavior; and that we need the help of a Higher Power to make these changes. Pages 56-57, 12 X 12

Bill W. points out another payoff of Step Five on page 58 of the 12 and 12, and that is that the experience deepens and strengthens our humility. Humility, later described as 'knowing that of ourselves we are nothing, the spirit within me does the work.' The first workable move toward experiencing the level of humility necessary to find recovery is to experience the depth of our defects and by admitting them to God, to ourselves and to another human being. After that we frequently experience another life changing surrender.

Once again, I want to mention the value of adding a fourth column to the inventory that is not described in the Big Book but was suggested by Joe and Charlie for the Fourth Step. Many people who have used a Fourth Column in the Fourth Step have told me that the greatest value in that process was their interaction with their sponsors in developing insight into their own behaviors. That being true, adding a Fourth Column to your Inventory during the Fifth Step would provide an even greater value because that includes a thorough and honest inventory of instances where you were resentful, selfish, dishonest, self-seeking, afraid, practiced selfish sex, and the in-depth questions and answers from the 12 and 12. It seems to me that a sponsor's insight into that depth of selfishness and self-centeredness would be most valuable if that assessment was made in the Fifth Step. Also, that would help the sponsee with his Sixth Step and later, when preparing for his amends.

My most recent 5th Steps have been with Bob B. and focused mostly on guidance for the sale of the Comedy club; and later on my resentments about having to sell the club and what amends I needed to make. Followed these 5th Steps, including related "Constructive Meditation," I had experienced important insights, two of which are noted as follows:

(1) When I was making my decisions on whether I should sell the business for a large amount of money I had not

even thought about asking for God's guidance. I knew that I didn't want to sell the business and was therefore certain that God also wanted us to keep it.

(2) Life is truly experienced in the NOW, with an ongoing personally satisfactory conscious partnership with God and it is essential to know this and to practice it on an ongoing basis.

Over the years Kenny S, George C., John H., Charles C. and Bob B. have all sponsored me. At no time in my sobriety have I not had a sponsor. I have done Fifth Steps with my last four sponsors. Each time I have deepened my feeling of connectedness with my Higher Power and with Alcoholics Anonymous. I think Pat and I and our kids are at the best place we have been.

Step Six

§

"Were entirely ready to have God remove
all these defects of character."

WHEN I WAS NEW IN AA it didn't take me long to see that the Program didn't really need 12 Steps. It only needed 10 Steps at the most. Steps 6 and 8 were simply 'Willingness Steps.' 'Getting Ready for the next Step,' Steps. "Willingness" was an essential part of every Step and it looked to me like Bill had wanted to have 12 Steps just to tie them in with the number of Disciples or something like that. I pretty much kept these 'insights' to myself because any 'original' thinking generally got me into trouble with someone.

Admittedly, the first few times I went through the Steps I more or less skipped the Seventh Step (which as I thought of then as *just a prayer*). I memorized the Prayer and said it with George C., John H., and my fourth sponsor Charles C., in Arizona, when we went through the Steps together. But, before coming to Arizona, I didn't really pray it or pay much attention to it so it did not take much effort for me to get ready for it.

I started my Sixth Step with the last full paragraph on Page 75 where Bill started Step Six in the Big Book. "Returning home we find a place where we can be quiet for an hour, carefully reviewing what we have done. We thank God from the bottom of our heart that we know Him better. (Actually taking the time to do this had a big payoff for me). "Taking this book down from our shelf we turn to the page which contains the twelve steps. Carefully reading the first five proposals we ask if we have omitted anything, for we are building an arch through which we shall walk a free man at last. Is our work solid so far? Are the stones properly in place? Have we skimped on the cement put into the foundation? Have we tried to make mortar without sand?"

Frank's guidance for me to be conscious in a meditative way when I read from the Big Book, "savoring every word and trying to take in the deep meaning of each phrase and idea. . . . " was essential for me in following these directions.

Logically relating and interweaving Meditation, Self-Examination and Prayer enabled me to center myself in the consciousness of the pervasive presence and power of God in my life and to then 'look for the deeper meaning of each word and phrase' as I reviewed Step One: "We admitted we were powerless over alcohol—that our lives had become unmanageable." I once again reviewed each part of the First Step; Part one: 'The loss of control of our drinking is characterized by the insane obsession each time that we start to drink that somehow, someway, this time we will control and enjoy our drinking, which allowed us to take the first drink; which is coupled with a physical reaction to alcohol and manifests itself in a phenomenon of craving for more once we start to drink, a craving much stronger than our will power to not take the next drink.' Then I asked myself: 'Have I omitted anything from this first part of the first step? Do I understand what characterizes alcoholism and being an alcoholic; do I fully concede to my inner most self that I am an alcoholic?' If I have done that I then look at part two of step one. . . . "We admitted that our lives had become unmanageable." Do I understand that 'selfishness and self-centeredness in the program means that we are like the actor who has to run the whole show? Do I understand that I lack the power to control everything so that everyone would be happy and everything would be wonderful...Do I see myself as the "victim of the delusion that I can wrest satisfaction and happiness out of this world if I only manage well?" Have I fully conceded to my inner-most self that I lack the power to manage my life so that I can wrest happiness and satisfaction out of this world. Have I done my best to "stop fighting everyone and everything, even alcohol?" If I am satisfied so far I then go to part three of step one: . . . "Our admissions of our personal powerlessness have become firm bedrock upon which I can build a happy comfortable life." Do I see that whatever power I have comes to me from a different source of power than myself; that fully conceding that truth to my inner most self acknowledges that I am personally powerless. If I have done my best to be open minded and acknowledge that I fit in each part of Step One, I then look at Step Two.

Again I become conscious of the 'deeper meaning of each word and phrase' in the second step: "Came to believe that a power greater than ourselves could restore us to sanity." I slowly and thoughtfully go over the elements of insanity that we acknowledged in the first step: 'the insane obsession that we can control and enjoy our drinking,' coupled with the insane '...delusion that we can wrest satisfaction and happiness out of this world if we only manage well." Then we focus on the Big Book ideas that: 'While none of us will ever completely comprehend or fully define this power, which is God;" we have come to believe that there is a "Spirit of the Universe under lying the totality of things;" which manifests "All-Powerful, Guiding, Creative Intelligence, Precise Law, order, harmony and goodness" in every aspect of all being; and that we have been given the power and the knowledge to effectively interact with the circumstances and events of our life, and to be conscious of our life's unfolding goodness. When I had done my best to accept the "three pertinent ideas: (a) That we were alcoholic and could not manage our own lives. (b) That probably no human power could have relieved our alcoholism. (c) That God could and would if He were sought." (Page 60, Big Book) Being convinced, we were at Step Three . . ."

I want to encourage you to take the Third Step in any way you feel is most effective for you. I have been pretty much following Frank's suggestions related to Bill's practice of "meditation, self-examination and Prayer, logically interrelated and interwoven," while praying the Third Step Prayer. I focus on the language and 'listen' for its deeper meaning and then stop from time to time and am conscious of what the next portion of the prayer might mean. Beginning the prayer as suggested in the Big Book by addressing: "God," (then pausing to be conscious of the pervasive presence of 'the Spirit of the Universe, having all-powerful, guiding, creative intelligence which manifests precise law, order and harmony underneath the material world and in life as we see it) "I offer myself to thee, to build with me and do with me as Thy wilt." (Here I stop and know that everything I need to fulfill my purpose will be drawn into my life today and I will be given the strength and knowledge to effectively interact with those circumstances and events, practicing patience, tolerance, kindness and love, and be conscious of my life's unfolding goodness. Knowing that truth and trusting it will "relieve me of the bondage of self that I may better do Thy will." (I then pause and know that the Spirit of the Universe does not experience problems, difficulties or unresolved circumstances; those experiences are the product of my thinking, my actions and my efforts to control things that I lack the power to control. And to know that God's Spirit only experiences order, harmony and unfolding goodness, which will): "Take away my difficulties that victory over them may bear witness to those I would help of Thy Power," (being conscious that that is all of the Power in the Universe), Thy Love, (Knowing that because The Spirit of God only experiences order, harmony and goodness in every aspect of all being, and therefore experience everything in Love. And to whatever extent I Love my Life I will be face to face with God's Love of my Life)," and Thy Way of Life," (Finally, knowing that God's way of life, at least, in part includes gracing His creation and His creatures with His Spirit for their goodness, then my way of life is best when I give of myself to God's creation and His creatures for their goodness). "May I do Thy will always." If I have stayed focused and sincerely prayed this prayer, and have not intentionally doubted its basic truth or left anything out, I go to the Fourth Step.

For my review of the Fourth Step, "Made a searching and fearless moral inventory of ourselves. . . I once again become conscious of the truth that I am a victim of the insane delusion that I can wrest happiness and satisfaction out of this world if I only manage well. Following that thought I can see that when people do not do what I want them to I become resentful of them; and I also see the most effective way to resolve each resentment is to acknowledge that of myself I do not have the power to forgive and to then seek help in finding this power. When I have forgiven the resentment I focus on knowing that that resentment has been forgiven and that I need to go on with my life. Now I consider those instances in my inventory where people responded to my efforts to manage them by caving in and giving me my way; generally because they do not want to have to endure my tirade if they didn't let me have my way. Here I need to see that having my own selfish, self-centered way, did not produce happiness and satisfaction, but instead caused feelings of regret, unworthiness and guilt. . . . Now I consider the instances where I behaved dishonestly; either through lying, cheating, stealing and self-deception and in a dishonest effort to force the outcome that my selfish and self-centeredness required for me to experience a sense of well-being. If I have deliberately left anything out I correct that before I go on to the next step, or satisfactorily resolve to ensure that that is done. . . . Next I satisfied myself that I have not left anything from my inventory about how I had jockeyed for a favorable position in self-seeking only for the purpose of helping me have my way; and, I satisfied myself that I did not want to continue that behavior and that I was willing to make amends where needed. . . . Then I considered my fear inventory. Have I left any of my fears out; and have I reviewed each fear by honestly asking myself 'why did I have them? Isn't it because self-reliance does not go far enough? Have I examined my fears in light of "…What if I had actually trusted God in each fearful situation?" When I was satisfied with my review, I was ready to go to my Sex inventory. . . . My sex inventory is really an inventory of all the 'short term' pleasures I seek that do not address my long term problems. Alcohol and drugs were my primary source of short term pleasure, but when I had to give those up I turned to sex, porn, gambling, money, authority, prestige, overeating, and the like. Hopefully, by this time i reached a point where I can see that the only effective solution to my long term living problems is to turn to a Higher Power in love and trust.

In Step Five "Admitted to God, to ourselves, and to another human being the exact nature of our wrongs," . . . I reviewed these words carefully, listening for a deeper meaning. Have I admitted to God and to myself the nature of my defects of character and have I listened for clarity and guidance in that process? Then, making certain that I have not knowingly left anything out of any of the Steps taken this far; especially in my admissions to another human being, I pause, and I ask ". . . if we have omitted anything, for we are building an arch through which we shall walk a free man at last. Is our work solid so far? Are the stones properly in place? Have we skimped on the cement put into the foundation? Have we tried to make mortar without sand? . . . If we can answer to our satisfaction, we then look at Step Six. We have emphasized willingness as being indispensable. Are we now ready to let God remove from us all the things which we have admitted objectionable? Can He now take them all—every one? If we cling to something we will not let go, we ask God to help us be willing." Page 76, Big Book

At this point I quietly visualized myself standing at a fork in the road of life: one path is the path of self-reliance and self-will, which has always been accompanied by resentments, self-ishness, self-seeking, dishonesty, fear and short term pleasures. The other path is supported by God reliance and God's will, which is accompanied by order, harmony and unfolding goodness. By comparing the nature, the character and quality that I know I found on the path of self-reliance, and considering the life promised on the path of God Reliance, I became willing to have God remove all of my defects of character.

While the Big Book's suggestions on a review of the first Five Steps provides a clear insight into our alcoholic problems and the willingness necessary to seek help in dispelling these problems, I found nothing in the Big Book's Sixth Step to prepare me for the opening statement on Step Six in the 12 and 12, which implies that it is Step Six that reveals the first major growth in spirituality. That any alcoholic who freely and truthfully repeatedly tries the Sixth Step on all their defects of character has demonstrated an unequivocal commitment to grow in the likeness of their Creator. Page 75 of the Big Book states that "We begin to feel the nearness of our Creator . . ." while taking our Fifth Step; but Step Six in the 12 and 12 tells us that the depth of that commitment is demonstrated by an ongoing commitment to working Step Six.

I am convinced that the insight we get from seeing "My Part" in the Fourth column of the Fifth Step will strengthen our readiness to let God take our defects of character from us.

As I have mention several times earlier it is in the 12 and 12 essay on Step Six where Bill W. most clearly emphasizes that when men and women drink enough alcohol to destroy their lives they are going against their fundamental desire for self-preservation. That these repeated beatings, administered by alcohol, may humble them so that grace will enter their lives and will smash the delusion that their drinking will ever be different; that someday they will once again control and enjoy their drinking. The smashing of that delusion results in the alcoholic being able to practice the first part of the First Step perfectly, while further strengthen themselves spiritually through working the next 11 Steps.

On the other hand, Bill highlights the fact that we cannot expect to have all (or any) of our defects of character completely expelled in the way our obsession to drink had been expelled. Step Six is AA's way of saying that we are beginning our lifelong commitment to surrendering our defects of character to God; and that once started we will continue to work towards perfect ideals. The words "entirely ready" highlight the fact that we are striving on an ongoing basis for growth in knowledge and performance. (Page 65, 12 and 12)

Bill W. makes another important clarification when he notes that the "key point" in the opening sentence in the Step Six essay which highlights that any alcoholic who openly, honestly and repeatedly tries Step Six on all their defects of character is demonstrating a commitment to growing in the likeness of their Creator and is clearly striving for the ***perfect goal***, rather than simply striving for ***what he thinks will get him by***. While our initial surrender was deep enough for us to practice 100 percent perfection in not taking the first drink, the best we could expect for the remaining 11 Steps was perfection as a standard for judgment; that that ideal would be the yardstick by which we could measure our success with the remaining 11 Steps. (Page 68, 12 and 12)

Once again in Step 6 of the 12 and 12 Bill wanted to emphasize that those of us who were completely beaten by alcohol and drugs and saw that we were alcoholics/addicts; that we had to stop drinking and using but that we were unable to do so through our own power and humbly turned for help. This surrender then allowed a power greater than ourselves to 'smash' the delusion that we could drink or use like normal people and were thereafter able to not take the next drink or drug, a day at a time, for the rest of our lives. Without that level of surrender we are unable to stop.

Similarly, the degree that we are able to let go of our resentments; selfishness; dishonesty; self-seeking; fear; obsessions with sex and other short term pleasures; money, property and prestige; positions of authority in our social life; and all other "children of the ego," depends directly on how "thoroughly and honestly" we work the Steps in order to see the depth of these defects in our character and at a level of humility deeper than our intellect surrender that "I didn't know I was this bad; I do not want to continue being this way but of myself I cannot help myself." Then, through the Seventh Step Prayer we ask for His help. Without *surrender* we are unable to grow at all.

In retrospect, I may have stayed sober without the Sixth Step but I am convinced that I would have remained angry, anxious and filled with dread 'long after the high tide of active alcoholism had receded.' It began to dawn on me that Father Dowling was absolutely right: that Step Six might well be the place where I was separated from many childhood ideas about myself, Life and God. I began to experience myself more as a spiritual man.

Step Seven

§

"Humbly asked Him to remove our shortcomings."

MY INITIAL ANALYSIS OF THE 12 Steps not only revealed that only 10 Steps were required for a full recovery from alcoholism, it also revealed that Step 7 should follow what is now Step 9, the Amends Step. Those changes should be clear to anyone who doesn't believe that God is really involved in their lives. If God is not in my life, I reasoned, I will have to make my amends myself. Then, I will be in spiritual shape to be willing that He should have all of me "good and bad."

In retrospect I can also see that my friendship with Frank was also important because he got me involved in Los Angeles Central Service work and helped me see that the Traditions were essential to AA's continued existence. That 'personal recovery indeed depended on AA Unity' and therefore, my sticking with the party line on the steps in their existing number and sequence would be my contribution to AA Unity. Also, as I noted earlier, my experience was that oldtimers and newcomers alike reacted badly to those members that shared important insights about the number and sequencing of the Steps.

I partly based my concerns about keeping my insights to myself on frequent discussions at Step Study meetings concerning the difference in the meaning of the phrases "defects of character" in Step 6; and "our shortcomings" in Step 7. These discussions were frequent and sometimes mildly "heated." I thought Chuck C. had resolved the problem In his Pala Mesa Talks in 1975 when he said "I bet you there've been a million hours spent in arguing over why Step Six says " . . . were entirely ready to have God remove all these defects of character . . ." and Step Seven says "humbly asked Him to remove our shortcomings." . . . Chuck C. then tells us that he asked Bill W. what the difference was and Bill had responded, "I don't know. I think I didn't want to end two lines right next to each other with the same words. They mean the same thing." I stayed out of it like a newcomer should because while I wanted attention, I didn't want it to be heated.

Later, when I actually read the Seventh Step Prayer and paid attention to the words, that question more or less resolved itself: "'My Creator, I am now willing that you should have all of me, good and bad. I pray that you now remove from me every single ***defect of character*** which stands in the way of my usefulness to you and my fellows. Grant me strength, as I go out from here, to do your bidding. Amen.' We have then completed *Step Seven*." (My emphasis on defect of character). Please take notice that I have kept my insight on this issue to myself until right now, as my continuing contribution to AA unity.

The Seventh Step Prayer is short but sweet. This prayer has transformed many sober lives in Alcoholics Anonymous. My third sponsor, John H., a former Catholic Priest, explained the humility that was apparent to him in the Seventh Step Prayer in a way that gave me a glimmer of what I eventually discovered in Bill W.'s Seventh Step Essay in the 12 and 12. John made special note that the prayer not only made clear that he could not remove defects of character without God's help he could not know which of them stood in the way of his usefulness to God and his fellows.

Very early in his essay on Step Seven in the 12 and 12 Bill notes that "Humbly". . . implies that 'Humility' plays a fundamental role in this Step and that we should pause for a moment and determine what that means to us in working the Step. He also notes that the achievement of deeper humility is a basic principle in each of AA's Twelve Steps.

So, let's look at a definition of humility that has been taken from the New Testament by both Chuck C. (*New Pair of Glasses*, Page 39) and Bill W. (12 X 12, Page 75): "Of myself I am nothing, the Father within doeth the works." When we actually found that our admissions of our personal powerless in Step One (12 X 12) was bedrock on which joyful and happy lives could be built, we made a great start in achieving deeper humility in our lives in the First Step; which is strengthen in each subsequent Step, building toward a deeper surrender in the other Eleven Steps.

In the Seventh Step essay Bill highlights the fact that AA does not belittle financial achievement and does not argue with those in our culture and our program who so vehemently hold to the conviction that getting what we want is the main goal of life. On the other hand, he points out that no group has ever made a worst shambles of their lives than alcoholics trying to satisfy their obsessions. He explained that after we are sober many of us demand more sex, money, property and prestige; coupled with more authority than we actually need or deserve. Again, both Chuck C. and Bill W. saw and argued that there was never enough of what we wanted to satisfy us. In every instance those of us that tried that way of life were held back by our lack of humility. Our egos stood in the way of our seeing the need for spiritual strength to come first, and that material success was not the purpose of life.

When, in AA, Bill points out, as we continued to deepen and broaden our experience of the Steps we saw failure and misery transformed by humility into happy and productive lives. We heard story after story of how humility had brought strength out of weakness. We began to recover from the mistaken belief that our Higher Power was to be called upon only in an emergency. The idea that we would still run our lives, calling on God only in emergencies, began to dissipate. But now the practice of humility, knowing that "Of myself I am nothing, the Father within doeth the works," began to promise an unshakeable foundation for living our lives.

We might once again consider that an alcoholic's brain chemistry is "spring loaded" to fight for having their way; but even when we have our way we do not feel pleasure, we feel 'fear of impending calamity.' Through working the Steps we gradually shut off the neural transmitters that activate the fight-or-flight center of the brain and gradually activate the neural transmitters that activate our sense of well-being. From 85 to 90 percent of the people in our culture do not have to work the Steps to experience a sense of well-being. But I am convinced that those alcoholics who diligently work the Steps end up with a better quality of life than that other 85 to 90 percent.

It is also important to understand that a life time spent fighting to have our way builds neural pathways on top of neural pathways guiding us to anger and anxiety. These pathways will not be changed by 'fighting with our egos'; our egos always win that battle. They will only change through surrender: "I now see that my life has been dominated by defects of character resulting in my basing my sense of well-being on my having my way; I know that will not work and I want to change; but I cannot change without help. My Creator, please help me."

When I ended Step Six, visualizing myself standing at a fork in the road of life, one path representing self-will and self-reliance, coupled with all my character defects; the other path representing God's Will and God Reliance, and promising a life of order, harmony and goodness if I would follow that path; I was conscious of my willingness to let God free me from my defects of character and I was ready to pray the Seventh Step Prayer from Page 76 of the Big Book.

So, slowly and thoughtfully, I prayed: "My Creator." . . . Pausing here to be conscious that I am addressing the Spirit that manifest the beginning of creation 13.7 billion years ago and continues in the on-going creation, manifesting All-Powerful, Guiding, Creative Intelligence, Precise Laws, Order, Harmony and Unfolding Goodness in every aspect of all being. . . . "I am now willing that you should have all of me, good and bad." . . . Pausing again to be conscious that every aspect of all being is in God's care and always has been; that my prayerful thought is an affirmation of what already is; 'that in and of myself I am nothing, It is the Father within than does the work;' and that 'nothing is either good or bad but thinking makes it so.' . . .

"I pray that you now remove from me every single defect of character which stands in the way of my usefulness to you and my fellows." . . . Pausing here to be conscious that I must rely on God to show me what defects stand between Him and I, and that I must be willing to take the path of God's will and God reliance, with its unfolding goodness, knowing that this path will lead me further into humility and freedom from self-will and the wreckage of my past, and to then consciously release myself into the care of my Creator. . . . "Grant me strength, as I go out from here to do your bidding."

Pausing here to be conscious that God gives me the strength and knowledge to do His will and to fulfill my purpose in life as one aspect of His unfolding Creation. . . . I say, "Amen."

Step Eight

§

**"Made a list of all persons we had harmed, and
became willing to make amends to them all."**

"NOW WE NEED MORE ACTION, without which we find that "Faith without works is dead." Let's look at Steps Eight and Nine. We have a list of all persons we have harmed and to whom we are willing to make amends. We made it when we took inventory. We subjected ourselves to a drastic self-appraisal. Now we go out to our fellows and repair the damage done in the past. We attempt to sweep away the debris which has accumulated out of our effort to live on self-will and run the show ourselves. If we haven't the will to do this we ask until it comes. Remember it was agreed at the beginning *we would go to any lengths for victory over alcohol.*" Page 76, Big Book

When I read that I said to myself "I do not remember agreeing to any such thing. I agreed to go to meetings and that was all I remember agreeing to. This is just Bill Wilson putting words in my mouth to get me to agree to something I was not going to agree to."

A few pages later in the Big Book I did read again: "Reminding ourselves that we have decided to go to any lengths to find a spiritual experience, we ask that we be given strength and direction to do the right thing, no matter what the personal consequences may be. . . . We must not shrink at anything. . . . Usually, however, other people are involved. Therefore, we are not to be the hasty and foolish martyr who would needlessly sacrifice others to save himself from the alcoholic pit." (Page 79, Big Book) Reading that I decided to give a little ground and while I would not admit I had agree to do this earlier I would agree to it now. Bill was probably not convinced that all (or perhaps even a majority) of the sober members remained angry, anxious, depressed and filled with dread long after the high tide of alcoholism had receded as described on pages 352 through 354 in the book "Pass It On." But he saw enough sober members who had to prompt him to turn to the writing of one essay for each Tradition and then one essay for each Step in the 12 and 12. And my experience in working each Step, first from the Big Book and then from the 12 and 12, in sequence, has been life changing in many special ways.

I am also convinced that the three column Fourth Steps enlarges on the thoroughness of the Fourth Step format over the Fourth column approach. I am also convinced that the value of the Fourth Column added to the inventory for the Fifth Step broadens and deepens the insight into what needs to be changed and amends to be made for newcomers and oldtimers alike.

Also, Step Eight is a great example of where Bill W. has taken a Step much deeper in the 12 X 12 than he did in the Big Book. I am convinced that most of us would benefit significantly from making a diligent effort to deepen and broaden our work on Step Eight as Bill has suggested in the 12 X 12. The Steps are indeed in the proper sequence to address our living problems.

You will notice that on Page 76 of the Big Book Bill wrote that "We have a list of all persons we have harmed and to whom we are willing to make amends. We made it when we took inventory." Now, on Page 77 of the 12 X 12 he explains that we had only partly prepared a list of persons we had harmed when writing our inventories, but we should now deepen and broaden our efforts to search out all the people and institutions we owed our amends. This certainly implies that we must "deepen and broaden" the Eighth Step if we are going to make real progress in finding a living answer to our living problems.

In redoubling our efforts what action does Bill suggest we take first? Initially we need to be willing to once again explore the need for forgiving the people, institutions or principles we have hurt by our selfish and self-centered behavior. The moment we examine damaged and distorted relationship we have had with others, we go on the defensive. To avoid acknowledging the wrongs we have done we resentfully focus on the wrong they have done us. This is especially true if they have actually harmed us in some way. Often we grab onto their behavior to justify the damage we have done them. Page 78, 12 X 12

Now, let's take another look at pages 66 and 67 in the Big Book: ". . . This was our course. We realized that the people who wronged us were perhaps spiritually sick." . . . "They, like ourselves, were sick too." . . . "We asked God to help us show them the same tolerance, pity (compassion), and patience that we would cheerfully grant a sick friend." . . . "We cannot be helpful to all people, but at least God will show us how to take a kindly and tolerant view of each and every one."

Somewhere along my road of recovery it occurred to me that what Bill is telling me here is that "tolerance, pity (compassion), patience and kindness" are for giving. But as I outlined in my Fourth Step experience with the 'sick man' prayer, I found needed insight about forgiveness from Emmitt Fox's essays on "The Lord's Prayer:" "Our true selves are at one with God, undivided from Him, expressing His ideas, witnessing to His nature--- the dynamic Thinking of that Mind." (Page 169) On that basis, I need God's help in doing this and I must ask for it. On Page 172, Emmet Fox also notes that,". . . nothing in all the world is easier than to forgive people who have not hurt us very much. Nothing is easier than to rise above the thought of some trifling loss." But if you have tried that and remain disturbed, ask for God's help in finding forgiveness. Because forgiveness not only puts the past into the past, it also shuts down that part of our nervous system that pumps the neuro-transmitters that activate the "Fight" center in the brain. The closing of the "Fight" center not only means relief from stress but opens the possibility of activating the "Pleasure" centers.

One brick wall we frequently encounter in making this survey is the realization that we are preparing to have a 'face to face' encounter with those we have hurt and to determine how we can repair that damage. Our old selfish behavior cries out, "I am not behaving that way now and I do not intend to revert to that old behavior. Why should I drag that up now?" Or, another obstacle is our insistence that we were only hurting ourselves. In my own case I would be immobilized with fear and remorse when I first woke up in the morning, but after a couple drinks in the "Tattle Tale" on my way to work I would think: "Why shouldn't I drink? It is necessary for me to have this feeling to do my job well. I am not hurting anyone else and I am paying the bills." The weakness of the latter argument was that I was not paying the bills. I was going deeper and deeper into debt and hiding that from Pat and everyone else. Such thinking is the basic result of denial, which as we now hear in meetings, "is no longer just a river in Egypt."

Inasmuch as our primary problem has been our defective relationship with the people, principles and institutions in our culture, Bill emphasizes that a close examination of this area of our lives will produce the most valuable results. Pages 79-80, 12 and 12

I took careful note of Bill's emphasis: Fear, the soul of the "Flight" center; and Pride, the soul of the ego, conspiring, not because there is any real danger to the self from making a list and becoming willing to make amends, but largely because we are spring loaded 'bio-chemically' to be afraid. And, the ego, of course, has always conspired to preserve itself as if it was really who we were.

I think it is helpful to me to be conscious of being resent-ful and angry; being afraid; and, being ego driven. I had stolen equipment from the equipment lab at work; every time I walked by the equipment lab fear of being caught pulled the 'life' out of me that I needed to live that moment. I owed Petrelli's Restaurant for dinners and drinks I had not paid for; and, every time I drove by Petrelli's I felt afraid and guilty, which also pulled the strength I needed to live that moment. The same thing was true about amends I owed Culver Motors Ford, my wife and kids, my boss, and on and on. As Bill noted, 'defective relations with other human beings have nearly always been the immediate cause of our woes. . . . The most effective way of ridding myself of the corresponding resentments, fears, and ego preservations, all of which stood between me and a conscious contact with God, was to be as honest and as thorough in working the Eighth and Ninth Steps as I could possibly be.

Now might also be a good time to pause and remind ourselves that Bill W. had nearly fifteen years to observe AA members failing to stay sober after they found AA; and observing that many of those who remained sober also remained angry, anxious, depressed and filled with dread when they encountered current problems in their lives. Seeing this, he recognized the need to 'broaden and deepen' the experience of oldtimers and newcomers alike in experiencing the 12 Steps in their lives. Thus he suggested a year by year walk back through our lives as far as memory will reach. We can prepare a long list of people who have, to some extent been affected. We shall want to hold ourselves to the course of forgiving the wrongs done to us and admitting the wrongs we have done to others. A calm, objective view will be our unwavering goal. Page 81-82, 12 X 12

I have always went over my amends list with my sponsor before making amends to assure that I was not falling on my sword in a way that would hurt my family or others. For the most part my sponsors have not asked me to change much about my planned amends.

Clearly, the Fourth Column you prepared with your sponsor as part of Step Five will also be valuable in preparing this list.

Step Nine

§

"Made direct amends to such people wherever possible,
except when to do so would injure them or others."

"PROBABLY THERE ARE STILL SOME misgivings. As we look over
the list of business acquaintances and friends we have hurt, we
may feel diffident abut going to some of them on a spiritual
basis. . . . At the moment, we are trying to put our lives in order.
But this is not an end in itself. Our real purpose is to fit ourselves to be of maximum service to God and the people around
us. It is seldom wise to approach an individual, who still smarts
from our injustice to him, and announce that we have gone
religious. . . . But our man is sure to be impressed with a sincere
desire to set right the wrong. He is going to be more interested
in a demonstration of good will than in our talk of spiritual
discoveries. " . . . "It may be he has done us more harm than we
have done him and, though we may have acquired a better attitude toward him, we are still not too keen about admitting our
faults. Nevertheless, with a person we dislike, we take the bit
in our teeth. . . . We go to him in a helpful and forgiving spirit,

confessing our *former* ill feeling and expressing our regret." Page 76-77, Big Book (my italics)

Note the words "former ill feeling" in the preceding sentence, implying that we have forgiven the other person before we express our regret for our own misbehavior.

"Before taking drastic action which might implicate other people we secure their consent. If we have obtained permission, have consulted with others (particularly your sponsor), asked God to help and the drastic step is indicated we must not shrink." Page 80, Big Book

"Yes, there is a long period of reconstruction ahead. We must take the lead. A remorseful mumbling that we are sorry won't fill the bill at all. We ought to sit down with the family and frankly analyze the past as we now see it, being very careful not to criticize them. Their defects may be glaring, but the chances are that our own actions are partly responsible. So we clean house with the family, asking each morning in meditation that our Creator show us the way of patience, tolerance, kindliness and love." . . . "The spiritual life is not a theory. *We have to live it*." . . . "There may be some wrongs we can never fully right. We don't worry about them if we can honestly say to ourselves that we would right them if we could. Some people cannot be seen---we send them an honest letter. . . . We should be sensible, tactful, considerate and humble without being servile or scraping. As God's people we stand on our feet; we don't crawl before anyone." Page 93, Big Book

In the 12 and 12 essays on Step Nine, Bill tells us that prudent judgment, thoughtful timing, and courage, are the attitudes we must have when we take Step Nine. As noted in Step

Eight, after we have made the list of people we have harmed, we thoughtfully reflect on each issue, generally with the guidance of our sponsor or spiritual advisor. We need to have the best spiritual attitude in which to proceed. In this way we can organize the amends to be made in terms of when and how they are to be done. There will be those amends that ought to be dealt with just as soon as we feel that we can maintain our sobriety. There will be cases where action ought to be deferred for various reasons, such as potential damage we may do to others by taking action too quickly. There will also be instances where the nature of the situation is such that we shall never be able to make direct personal contact at all. Frequently we begin making direct amends on the day we join Alcoholics Anonymous.

The moment we tell our family that we have joined AA, the process has begun. At this first family meeting we should start with a general admission of our defects. It may be unwise to go into any detail about our drunken behavior. These same guidelines will apply at the office or factory. First we will want to be reasonably certain that we are in fact ready to make the necessary commitment to sobriety and the AA program of action. Then we are ready to go to these people, to tell them what AA is, and what we are trying to do. We can acknowledge the damage we have done and make our amends. We can pay, or make satisfactory arrangements to pay, whatever obligations we owe. Page 83-84, 12 X 12

There may be one consideration which should modify our desire to fully disclose the damage we have done. That will arise where making a full disclosure would harm the one to whom we are making amends. Or---just as important---someone else.

The question about making such amends should be placed before our sponsor or spiritual advisor, earnestly asking God's help and guidance---meanwhile resolving to do the right thing when it becomes clear, regardless of the cost to ourselves. Page 86-87, 12 X 12

When I first got sober, everywhere I went I ran into people, places and things that were a source of fear and guilt because of amends I needed to make. Actually it took me several iterations through the steps before I backed out of ongoing anger and anxiety and began to experience the goodness of my life on an ongoing basis. The first time through the steps I got to the tall poles in the tent mostly from my childhood. I forgave my dad for having abused me physically and emotionally and I paid off $2,500.00 in debts at the Bank of America and Company Credit Union that Pat didn't know about. I then told her about them. I took the equipment back that I had stolen from work and set me up as a candidate for hard time in a federal penitentiary. I paid Petrelli's Restaurant and all the other "small debts" that I had regarded as 'nothing' until I found that paying them off set me free to live my life in the now. Finally, I told Pat the truth about every lie I could remember and I stopped lying to her. Soon after that she told me that she would stop threatening to leave me and we would work harder to solve our problems.

The payoff for cleaning up all of the wreckage of the past was essential to my being able to feel good about my life. The morning after I took the test equipment back and they let me off the hook for stealing it, I woke up and realize this was off my back and I felt as good as I had when I had my first drink of whiskey: No anxiety and very active pleasure centers. I believe that Bill W. was following Spiritual guidance when he wrote the Steps for them to specifically address the biochemistry in exactly the right sequence and increments.

Another important 9th Step experience for me happened when I was 13 years sober. Clancy I. asked Jim S., the Chairman of the first Mt. High AA conference, to invite me to be the Sunday Morning speaker at that conference. I had always been quietly critical of some of the activities in the Pacific Group, but Frank G. had advised me to keep that criticism to myself. One of the activities I was critical of was their 'sing along.' After the Friday Night Speaker was through, the speaker (Jim W. of Ft. Worth, Texas) and I sat together in the conference dining hall. With Clancy playing the piano, the entire attendance sang along. I knew all the lyrics to every song they sang and I sang with them. When we were singing "Blue Eyes Crying in the Rain," I re-experienced setting under the kitchen table in our home in Milan, Kansas, when I was about 6 years old, looking through the crocheted hole of my mom's best table cloth and watching Foster Meyers, a musician friend of my dad's, sing that song. My dad had a country band playing at our house frequently, and while I didn't realize it at the time, that music had become a therapy for me. That night at the conference I had a very good feeling about my dad bringing that music into my life. The next day at the softball tournament, an activity that I also silently criticized, I had a similar experience and realized that my dad had agreed to manage the Argonia Town Team baseball team so I could be the bat boy. I again felt good about my dad and I realized that while I had forgiven dad in my Fourth Step, I had never felt good about him or my childhood, and that these experiences this weekend were special experiences for me. After I returned to Phoenix after the Conference, the Voice (or a thought) came to me: "You were given two freebees about the goodness of your dad in your life this last weekend. Perhaps if you would put effort into it you would find other goodness he brought into your life."

I established a meditation practice for when I got home from an evening meeting where I would focus on some good thing dad had done for us kids. I found a bunch of things, for example, he built a basketball goal and court in our back yard. He put the Lyric Theater's movie poster on our barber shop building in exchange for tickets to the Sunday night movie. We frequently went to the Wichita Park and Zoo for picnics and baseball games. We went fishing and hunting. He built high jump and pole vault standards for us boys to practice on. He took me with him to town teams games of all kinds. He frequently popped popcorn in the evening and made ice cream on Sunday afternoons.

One evening I was fanaticizing myself as a kid practicing high jumping into the sand pit when I lost control of my fantasy. All at once I experienced going out of the back of the house right after dad had whipped me. I was crying and could not get my breath. In this fantasy I imagined that I hugged the little kid and told him that everything is going to turn out better than it looked like it would. Then, I felt myself being hugged. I looked up and it was my dad hugging me and the little kid, with the most loving expression on his face and he was crying. My feeling about my dad and my childhood changed that moment. Since then I have been conscious of having had a really good childhood in which I was whipped too hard three times that I could remember. Those whippings must have been traumatic, and the meditations had "amended" my feelings about my childhood and my dad. I also believe that in this instance I had somehow experienced a level of humility much deeper than my intellect that allowed God to enter my life and expel my belief that I had a bad childhood.

I recently experienced another amends related to the above story. When I was in High School I would steal money out of my dad's cash drawer. I don't know how much money I had taken. My dad died sober at an AA meeting on March 8, 1951, when I was in Korea. I simply overlooked that amends until my mom had passed and I had a low grade feeling of regret that I didn't make the amends with her. Recently, in a meeting where a fellow member was sharing about his Ninth Step experiences the thought came to me that my experience with my dad in that meditation included our amends for all wrongs done by either and both of us. As frequently happens in those experiences, a good feeling started just above my ankles, slowly rose up through my body, leaving goose bumps on the back of my hands and neck. I thought of Frank and His God letting me know He felt my amends and that He had my back.

I need to work every step to the best of my ability, but the Ninth Step has been of major importance in changing my life. I have started going over all the Steps as I prepared this guide to the 12 Steps. I am especially focused on the Eighth Step as described in the 12 X 12 and then on making my amends. This has certainly served as a basis for me to be a better husband.

Amending my life has included instances such as listening to Dr. Paul describe how he fixed his wife Max coffee every morning. It was a funny story but also a sad one for me.

"I don't do much for you." I told Pat after the meeting. "I am going to start fixing you coffee in the morning."

Pat frowned at me and replied "I have tasted your coffee and it isn't that great. Why don't you massage my feet once in a while?"

That conversation took place a couple years before Dr. Paul passed on. At first I massaged Pat's feet a couple of times a week but she told me she would like to limit the massage to once a week. "That way it will remain special."

I am still massaging her feet nearly every Tuesday night. I give each foot a half hour massage. Some weeks, when she is especially tired or her feet are swollen, I massage them a couple times that week.

In August of 2012 Pat had a series of health problems that resulted in two strokes and the loss of her eye sight. During our first 59 years of marriage Pat had taken care of our entire family. I mean she helped us all in wonderful ways in everything we were doing. At the start of her illnesses in August of 2012 we had an almost complete reversal of roles. At first, all of my time involved my being her caregiver. In terms of amending behaviors this required me to make tremendous changes in my thinking and behavior. Our daughter Anne has also been a super supporter and caregiver to both Pat and I. Gradually, as Pat's health has continued to improve she has been able to do many things without our help, but we remain her caregivers. My ability to respond to help her overcome these problems is completely the result of the 12 Steps and resulting spiritual strength they have brought me.

Recently, our daughter, Anne, in describing someone else's poor behavior said, "He acts just like dad used to." I took that as a major compliment.

"If we are painstaking about this phase of our development, we will be amazed before we are half way through. We are going to know a new freedom and a new happiness. We will not regret the past nor wish to shut the door on it. We will comprehend the word serenity and we will know peace. No matter how far down the scale we have gone, we will see how our experience can benefit others. That feeling of uselessness and self-pity will disappear. We will lose interest in selfish things and gain interest in our fellows. Self-seeking will slip away. Our whole attitude and outlook upon life will change. Fear of people and of economic insecurity will leave us. We will intuitively know how to handle situations which used to baffle us. We will suddenly realize that God is doing for us what we could not do for ourselves." Page 83-84, Big Book

Step Ten

§

"Continued to take personal inventory and when
we were wrong promptly admitted it."

As I HAVE MENTIONED, I was not going to work the Steps at all when I first came to the Program. Then I gradually 'came to believe' that I had taken the First Step when I came and stayed in AA. Leo H., who had the second longest sobriety in my home group, had invariably insisted that working the First and Twelfth Steps were all we really needed do to stay sober. At one time in my early sobriety I decided to follow his guidance. (Leo was actually a very important link in my continued growth. It now seems that everyone was in some way.) My life continued to get better every day. I stayed in the program but it wasn't getting better fast enough for me. Nevertheless, 'those middle Steps' with the written inventory, the admitting bad behavior to another human being, and then making amends for my wrongs was clearly not something I wanted to do. I did not think that doing that stuff was going to make my life better.

A not too careful reading of the following paragraph from the Big Book convinced me that I should start doing a daily inventory to keep my slate clean each day. I saw that in the long run that would eventually allow me to let the 'past bury the past' and for me to live my life 'One Day at a Time." So, I decided to expand my program to Three Steps: One, Twelve and Ten.

"This thought brings us to Step Ten, which suggests we continue to take personal inventory and continue to set right any new mistakes as we go along. We vigorously commenced this way of living as we cleaned up the past. We have entered the world of the Spirit. Our next function is to grow in understanding and effectiveness. This is not an overnight matter. It should continue for our lifetime. Continue to watch for selfishness, dishonesty, resentment, and fear. When these crop up, we ask God at once to remove them. We discuss them with someone immediately and make amends quickly if we have harmed anyone. Then we resolutely turn our thoughts to someone we can help. Love and tolerance of others is our code." Page 84, Big Book

Inasmuch as Bill uses the word continue and continued four times in the foregoing sentences I looked it up in my Webster's: "Continue: to maintain without interruption a condition, course or action." It seems to suggest that we start something and simply keep doing it in an ongoing basis, thereby building new brain circuits through neuroplasticity.

The paragraph quoted above from page 84 of the Big Book has been one of the most helpful to me in finding my sobriety. I think this Step, as worded: "Continued to take personal inventory and when we were wrong promptly admitted it" . . . understates what is really involved with Step 10.

The sentence: "We vigorously commenced this way of living *as* we cleaned up the past." (My emphasis added) The word *as* implies to me that we should start this step when we start the Fourth Step, which is the beginning of cleaning up the past. This makes sense to me in that we would be in something similar to an infinite regression if we didn't start "cleaning up the present" when we started cleaning up the past.

The next two sentences: "We have entered the world of the Spirit. Our next function is to grow in understanding and effectiveness." In the Fifth Step Bill wrote that "We begin to feel the nearness of our Creator." In the Seventh Step we are ". . . now willing that you should have all of me, good and bad." In the Ninth Step "We will suddenly realize that God is doing for us what we could not do for ourselves."

Now, "We have entered the world of the Spirit." I found that I had to actually 'grow in understanding and effectiveness' before I could effectively watch for selfishness, dishonest, resentment and fear.' For certain the last sentence in this paragraph: "Love and tolerance of others is our code" . . . had to find its way into my consciousness before I could really get any kind of foothold on a spiritual way of living.

"It is easy to let up on the spiritual program of action and rest on our laurels. We are headed for trouble if we do, for alcohol is a subtle foe. We are not cured of alcoholism. What we have is a daily reprieve contingent on the maintenance of our spiritual condition. Every day is a day when we must carry the vision of God's will into all of our activities. 'How can I best serve Thee---Thy will (not mine) be done.' These are thoughts which must go with us constantly. We can exercise our will power along this line all we wish. It is the proper use of the will." Page 85, Big Book.

Remember that when Bill wrote this paragraph he knew nothing about the process of neuroplasticity. But the actions he describes are essential to causing and keeping active new 'spiritual' brain circuits.

In Bill's essay on the Tenth Step, in the 12 X 12 he notes that although all inventories are alike in principle; the timing distinguishes one from the other. There's the spot check inventory that we take as we go through the day and find ourselves upset by current circumstances and events. There's the inventory we take when we retire at night. Then there are the inventories that we take when alone, or with our sponsor or spiritual adviser, when we review of our progress as dictated by recent events or circumstances. Many of us do annual inventories or take an occasional retreat from our busy lives where we can be quiet for a weekend of talk, prayer and meditation. Page 89, 12 X 12

It is a spiritual law that when we are upset, no matter what the cause; there is something wrong with us. We have found that anger, jealousy, envy, self-pity, or hurt pride should be addressed by a spot-check inventory taken in the midst of such experiences. 'Easy Does It' is the answer in these instances. Here we need self-restraint, an objective look at what is involved, a willingness to admit when the fault is ours, and an equal willingness to forgive when the fault is elsewhere. Our first spiritual goal will be self-restraint. One unkind tirade or one willful snap judgment can ruin our relation with another person for a day, a year or a lifetime. As noted by Henry Drummond in his essays on St. Paul's letters to the Corinthians, we must avoid quick-tempered criticism as well as quiet scorn. "For the want of kindness, a want of generosity, a want of courtesy, a want of unselfishness, are all instantaneously symbolized in one flash of temper." (Page 37) As we continue to work the Steps, we will find that with God's help we develop the needed neural pathways of self-restraint. These pathways are put into place; but we have to take the action.

When I first came to the program I was not going to work the Steps at all. Then in a short time, Leo H., our resident two stepper, would proclaim, "I have stayed sober and lived a happy life for 24 years just working the First and Twelfth Steps." That made a lot of sense to me and I decided to do the same thing. After a few months of that it occurred to me that while I was never going to do a Fourth or Fifth Step, nor would I do the Eighth or Ninth, that it would be a good thing to do a daily inventory and not build up any new problems in my life. I could live life a day at a time, accepting all my past resentments and amends, if I didn't add to that list. In that way I would be a three stepper: First, Tenth and Twelfth Steps would be my Program.

You know my story about deciding to quit AA (a frequently made decision whenever I was not having my way) on a Saturday afternoon, and Saturday night hearing Don G. say: "If you are not working the Steps and you stop going to meetings, then you will go to the bar for a drink. If the bartender asks, 'I thought you were going to AA. Don't AA work?' Be honest and admit that you don't know if AA works or not, because you didn't try." On my way home that night I decided to work *all* the Steps.

Looking back at the first paragraph quoted on the Tenth Step from the Big Book: I tried to follow the direction,". . .

Continue to watch for selfishness, dishonesty, resentment, and fear. When these crop up, we ask God at once to remove them. . . ." I continued my efforts to follow that direction for months, although to the best of my knowledge and memory I was not able to actually do that successfully one time. *NOT ONE TIME.* The best I was able to do was to make a feeble amends if I had harmed someone. My wife (or my boss) for example, was not impressed with my promise to do better after I failed time and time again to do better.

Near the end of my First AA Birthday Frank had started to teach me to pray and meditate from Step 11 in the 12 X 12. I got off to a typical stop and go start but by October 1974 I was committed to meditate for 30 minutes every day on something, for six months. Then, on April First of the next year, I would change to something else for the next six months. Sometime along the way I heard Bob C. (Sybil's last husband; she had many) tell his story. Bob had spent some time in prison for armed robbery, and while in prison he attended AA meetings.

His prison AA group had focused on practicing LOVE as described in Henry Drummond's little book "The Greatest Thing in the World." Drummond had used St. Paul's letter on love in 1 Corinthians, 13 Chapter as the text for writing this valedictory address for a group of graduating missionaries. My mother had actually left that little book to me when she passed away but I didn't read it because it was biblical. Bob C. convinced me that it was part of the literature Dr. Bob asked his sponsee's to read, along with Fox's Sermon on the Mount, The Lord's Prayer, and other spiritual writings. I decided to take the "risk" and read it. However, I was literally fearful of getting caught up again in biblical teachings. Actually that little book had a transforming effect on me. It is short and could easily be read in an evening. I read it over several times and then decided to memorize and meditate on 1st Cor. 13th Chapter and on parts of *"The Greatest Thing in the World."*

Basically, after memorizing First Corinthians my meditation was to be conscious of the 'deeper' meaning of each word and phrase as I repeated it to myself. It is essentially composed of three parts; and my goal was to get through the first part without my mind wandering. Then I would focus on the second part without my mind wandering. If my mind wandered from the text I had to start that part over again. When I made it through the second part I could then focus on the third part and get through it without losing my place. Then I would go over each of the elements of love as it is described by Drummond in his little book. The actual text that I meditated on was:

"Though I speak with the tongues of men and of angels, and have not Love, I am become as sounding brass, or a tinkling cymbal. And though I have the gift of prophecy, and understand all mysteries, and all knowledge; and though I have all faith, so that I could remove mountains, and have not Love, I am nothing. And though I bestow all my goods to feed the poor, and though I give my body to be burned, and have not love, it profiiteth me nothing."

"Love suffereth long, and is kind; Love envieth not; Love vaunteth not itself, is not puffed up, doth not behave itself unseemly, seeketh not her own, is not easily provoked, thinketh no evil; Rejoiceth not in iniquity, but rejoiceth in truth; Beareth all things, believeth all things, hopeth all things, endureth all things."

"Love never faileth; but whether there be prophecies, they shall fail; whether there be tongues, they shall cease; whether there be knowledge, it shall vanish away. For we know in part and we prophesy in part. But when that which is perfect is come then that which is in part shall be done away. When I was a child, I spake as a child, I understood as a child, I thought as a child; but when I became a man, I put away childish things. For now we see through a glass, darkly; but then face to face: now I know in part; but then shall I know even as also I am known. And now abideth faith, hope, Love these three; but the greatest of these is Love."

Having worked my way through St. Paul, I then focused on these excerpts from the little book:

". . . Paul passes this thing, Love, through the magnificent prism of his inspired intellect, and it comes out on the other side broken up into its elements. . . . The Spectrum of Love has nine ingredients:"

"Love suffereth long." "Love is patience. This is the normal attitude of Love; Love passive, Love waiting to begin; not in a hurry; calm; ready to do its work when the summons comes. . . . Love suffers long, beareth all things, believeth all things, hopeth all things. For Love understands, and therefore waits."

"And is kind." "Love is kindness. Love active. 'The greatest thing a man can do for his Heavenly Father is to be kind to some of His other children.' 'I will pass through this world but once. Any good thing therefore that I can do or any kindness that I can show to any human being, let me do it now. Let me not defer it or neglect it, for I shall not pass this way again.'"

"Love envieth not." "Love is generosity. If I love my life, as God Loves my life, then if some great good thing happens to someone else I will rejoice in that; nothing needs to change in my life when I Love my life as God Loves my life."

"Love vaunteth not itself, is not puffed up." "Love is humility. After you have been kind, after Love has stolen forth into the world and done its beautiful work, go back into the shade again and say nothing about it. Love hides even from itself. Love waives even self-satisfaction. "

"Doth not behave itself unseemly." "Love is courtesy. This is Love in society, Love in relation to etiquette. Politeness has been defined as love in trifles. Courtesy is said to be love in little things. And the one secret of politeness is to Love. Love cannot behave itself unseemly."

"Seeketh not her own." "Love is unselfishness. . . . The more difficult thing still is not to seek things for ourselves at all. . . . Why? Because there is no greatness in things. . . . there is no happiness in having and getting anything, but only in giving. I repeat, there is no happiness in having, or in getting, but only in giving."

"Love is not easily provoked." "Love is good tem-per. Temper is significant. . . . It is a test for love, a symptom, a revelation of an unloving nature at bot-tom. It is the intermittent fever which bespeaks inter-mittent disease within; the occasional bubble escaping to the surface which betrays some rottenness under-neath. . . . For a want of patience, a want of kindness, a want of generosity, a want of courtesy, a want of unselfishness, are all instantaneously symbolized in one flash of temper."

"Thinketh no evil." "Love is guilelessness. Guilelessness is the grace for suspicious people. Love 'thinketh no evil,' imputes no motive, sees the bright side, put the best con-struction on every action. . And if we try to influence or elevate others, we shall soon see that success is in propor-tion to their belief of our belief in them."

"Love rejoiceth not in iniquity, but rejoiceth in the truth." "I have called this Sincerity. . . . It includes, perhaps more strictly, the self-restraint which refuses to make capital out of others' faults; the charity which delights not in exposing the weakness of others, but "covereth all things;" the sincerity of purpose which endeavors to see things as they are, and rejoices to find them better than suspicion feared or calumny denounced."

I did not memorize these quotes from Drummond's book, but I learned them and would go over each one as I went through St. Paul's Letter on Love. I don't know how long it took me but someplace in my six month commitment to this meditation I began to experience a deeper meaning of the words and ideas in these writings. I also began to consciously experience loving my life, my wife, my work, and the people around me in a new way. I also began taking each element (in the sequence set by St. Paul: Patience, Kindness, Generosity, Humility, etc.) and committed myself to practicing that element of Love in my life that day. Then I discovered that by focusing on the last sentence of the quote from page 84 of the Big Book, "Love and tolerance of others is our code. . ." and being conscious of loving my life, I was able to effectively ". . . watch for selfishness, dishonesty, resentment, and fear. When these crop up . . ." I could avoid them by going to whatever element of Love I was practicing that day." I am not perfect at this but it has made a major, major difference in my working the Tenth Step and in living my life.

Over time I have discovered that I cannot get very far away from being conscious of loving my life in my meditation and remain at peace. Currently I practice a 30 minute or more slowed down version of the Third Step Prayer in the morning and evening, and when I close that prayer with: ". . . of Thy power, (I stop and am conscious that the Spirit of the Universe has *All-Powerful*, Guiding, Creative Intelligence, underlying every aspect of all being;) Thy Love, (I stop here and know that the Spirit of God only experiences order, harmony and unfolding goodness, and experiences that in Love. If I Love my own life as God loves my life I am face to face with God, who is also Love. I then go over Drummond's description of the element of love for that day and commit to consciously practicing that element of Love in my life throughout the day. Any one or all of those elements are appropriate responses to replace selfishness, dishonesty, resentment, and fear, "when these crop up." . . . "and Thy way of life." (I stop here and know that God's way of life includes gracing the Universe with His Spirit for the good of His creation and creature; and that my best way of life would therefore be to give myself in service to God's creation and creatures for their goodness.) "May I do Thy Will Always. Amen"

I suspect that I have always been troubled with Attention Deficit Disorder of some kind. Much of my misbehavior when I was a kid was stuff I would never have done if I would have been aware of what I was doing instead of "day dreaming." Things like punching the blisters on the wall paper behind where the German Heater stood during the winter; and then peeling the paper off the wall. I was smarter than to do that if I had been conscious that I was doing it. I knew that that would get me an "ass whipping" but I didn't realize I was doing it until it was done. Then, sure enough, came the "ass whippings."

In some ways I am just as 'absent minded' as I ever was. I see something I need to do, like picking up the shorts I had left on the floor last night. Through most of our married life Pat would pick them up and put them in the cloth's hamper. Frequently, if Pat was on a trip somewhere and I was home by myself, after a couple days of my shorts just lying there I would wonder why they were still there. Then it would dawn on me that she always picks them up for me. I might pick them up then, but when she returned, that became her job again.

Today, I am making a concerted effort to be in the now and when I see that something needs to be done, to do it now. The fact that I see the need to make that effort is a major change that has come to me from the Tenth Step. I have not specifically read this anywhere in my research, but it has occurred to me that if I am "Attention Deficit Disordered" that that might stem from childhood neural pathways that could be addressed by the Neural plasticity embedded in the Twelve Steps. I am becoming convinced of that "A Day at a Time."

Step Eleven

§

"Sought through prayer and meditation to improve our conscious contact with God as we understood Him, praying only for knowledge of His will for us and the power to carry that out."

ONCE AGAIN, CONSIDERING THAT WITH the Fifth Step we begin to feel the nearness of our Creator; with the Seventh Step we become willing for God to have all of us, good and bad; with the Ninth Step we begin to see how God is doing for us what we could not do for ourselves; and then, with the Tenth Step we enter the world of the Spirit; if we are not diligent with the Eleventh Step we will be missing the 'payoff' of the program: *"improving our conscious contact with God and being conscious of His will for us and having the power to carry that out."* The Big Book says the following:

". . . So we clean house with the family, asking each morning in meditation that our Creator show us the way of patience, tolerance, kindliness and love." Page 83

"... Every day is a day when we must carry the vision of God's will into our activities. 'How can I best serve Thee---Thy will (not mine) be done.' These are thoughts which must go with us constantly. We can exercise our will power along this line all we wish. It is the proper use of the will." ... "Step Eleven suggests prayer and meditation. We shouldn't be shy on this matter of prayer. Better men than we are using it constantly. It works, if we have the proper attitude and work at it." Page 85-6

"On awakening let us think about the twenty-four hours ahead. We consider our plans for the day. Before we begin, we ask God to direct our thinking, especially asking that it be divorced from self-pity, dishonest or self-seeking motives." ... "In thinking about our day we may face indecision. We may not be able to determine which course to take. Here we ask God for inspiration, an intuitive thought or a decision. We relax and take it easy." Page 86

"As we go through the day we pause, when agitated or doubtful, and ask for the right thought or action. We constantly remind ourselves we are no longer running the show, humbly saying to ourselves many times each day "Thy will be done." We are then in much less danger of excitement, fear anger, worry, self-pity, or foolish decisions." Page 87-88

NOTE: Inasmuch as Bill W. used the word 'constantly' three times within those few pages, I looked it up in my Webster's. 'Constantly. Something invariable or unchanging.' "Why it is almost like 'continue' in the Tenth Step," Dr. Paul might say.

We usually conclude the period of meditation with a prayer that we be shown all through the day what our next step is to be, that we be given whatever we need to take care of such problems. We ask especially for freedom from self-will, and are careful to make no request for ourselves only." . . . "If not members of religious bodies, we sometimes select and memorize a few set prayers which emphasize the principles we have been discussing. There are many helpful books also." . . . "Be quick to see where religious people are right. Make use of what they offer." Page 87, Big Book

"When we retire at night, we constructively review our day. Were we resentful, selfish, dishonest or afraid? Do we owe an apology? Have we kept something to ourselves which should be discussed with another person at once? Were we kind and loving toward all? What could we have done better? Were we thinking of ourselves most of the time? Or were we thinking of what we could do for others, of what we could pack into the stream of life? But we must be careful not to drift into worry, remorse or morbid reflection, for that would diminish our usefulness to others. After making our review we ask God's forgiveness and inquire what corrective measures should be taken." Page 86, Big Book

"It works---it really does." Page 88, Big Book

"We alcoholics are undisciplined. So we let God discipline us in the simple way we have just outlined." Page 88, Big Book

In summary, the Big Book suggests that we pray and meditate as part of working every Step, upon awakening, in planning our day, when facing indecision, as we go through the day when we are agitated or doubtful, "We constantly remind ourselves we are no longer running the show," "Better men than we are using it (prayer) constantly. . . ." "'How can I best serve Thee---Thy will (not mine) be done.' These are thoughts that must go with us constantly. . . ." and, when we retire at night. While the Big Book clearly reveals that prayer and meditation is the hub of our program, it says little about how to pray and meditate.

As with all of the Steps, before using this guide on how to 'deepen and broaden' Step 11 after working it from the Big Book, I suggest you carefully read Step 11 from the 12 and 12.

Now, after you have read Step 11 in the 12 and 12, I want to try to orient you like Frank tried to orient me. First off, I know Frank loved the St. Francis Prayer, and spent hours going over it. But by the same token, it is a Saint's Prayer. In retrospect, I had around one year of sobriety at the time, and Frank thought I would have little (say No) success in actually gaining much Spiritual Strength from the St. Francis Prayer until I had worked my way through the 12 Steps and actually had some kind of a Spiritual Awakening. And, that I needed some kind of Prayer and Meditation practice to make it through the 12 Steps. So, when Frank was trying to teach me to Pray and Meditate he first focused me on the idea that prayer and meditation are '. . . our principle means of conscious contact with God. . .' and, then on logically relating and interweaving the Steps through meditation, self-examination and prayer.

As structured by Bill W., and suggested by Frank, in Part 1, Step 1, I conceded my powerless over alcohol; in Part 2, Step 1, I conceded that I lacked the power to control the outcome of the circumstances and events of my life so I cannot depend on having my way as a reliable sense of well-being; and, Part 3, Step 1, written years after the Big Book, I admitted that I was personally powerless. To me, this admission did in fact serve as a 'bed rock' on which I could build a happy comfortable life with reliance on a Spirit of the Universe having: All Powerful, Guiding, Creative Intelligence. . . "

Now I want to include a discussion from Aldous Huxley's book, "The Perennial Philosophy" which I think is responsive to Bill W.'s questions in the above paragraph; and, which I think is worth considering when we are petitioning God to give us what we want. Huxley might be speaking from his own experience, but he was certainly speaking for me in the way I was taught to pray when I was a 'baby elephant.' But before I get into quoting Huxley let me quote my Webster's:

Meditation is defined as "Contemplation."

Contemplation is defined as: "(a) Concentration on spiritual things as a form of private devotion. (b) a state of mystical awareness of God's being."

So on to Mr. Huxley. He writes,

"The word 'prayer' is applied to at least four distinct procedures—petition, intercession, adoration, contemplation. Petition is the asking of something for ourselves. Intercession is the asking of something for other people. Adoration is the use of intellect, feeling, will and imagination in making acts of devotion directed towards God in his personal aspect or as incarnated in human form. Contemplation is that condition of alert passivity, in which the soul lays itself open to the divine

Ground within and without, the immanent and transcendent Godhead." . . . "Psychologically, it is all but impossible for a human being to practice contemplation without preparing for it by some kind of adoration and without feeling the need to revert at more or less frequent intervals to intercession and some form at least of petition. On the other hand, it is both possible and easy to practice petition apart not only from contemplation, but also from adoration and, in rare cases of extreme and unmitigated egotism, even from intercession. Petitionary and intercessory prayer may be used---and used, what is more, with what would ordinarily be regarded as success---without any but the most perfunctory and superficial reference to God in any of his aspects. To acquire the knack of getting his petitions answered, a man does not have to know or love God, or even know or love the image of God in his own mind. All that he requires is a burning sense of the importance of his own ego and its desires, coupled with a firm conviction that there exists, out there in the universe, something not himself which he wheedled or dragooned into satisfying those desires. If I repeat "My will be done," with the necessary degree of faith and persistency, the chances are that, sooner or later and somehow or other, I shall get what I want. Whether my will coincides with the will of God, and whether in getting what I want I shall get what is spiritually, morally or even materially good for me are questions which I cannot answer in advance. "Page 219-20, Aldous Huxley, *"The Perennial Philosophy"*

Although I do not fully agree with the last part of Huxley's comments, I have had very little success with petitional prayers; and I gave them all I had in terms of self-will. Early in my efforts to follow the guidance in Step 11 of the 12 X 12. When I came to the end of the first Step, Frank suggested that I stop there for a moment and be open to an awareness of how the problems that had brought me to the program had all been solved and to also be aware of what little I had to do with that outcome. Then he told me that the definition for grateful was a ". . . feeling of appreciation for benefits received;" and if I felt that, one prayer would be to simply say "Thank you God."

But he quickly added: "I don't want you to say that prayer."

He then touched his cup and said, "This is not a cup."

He touched his chair, "This is not a chair."

He touched the table and said, "This is not a table." "Cup, chair and table are words; these objects are not words they are what they are. And, 'Thank you God' is just words. . . . If you feel grateful, let that feeling be your prayer. And, if you then have a good feeling with goose bumps coming up your legs, body, back of the hands and neck that will be my God saying: "I felt your gratitude and you are welcome."

Years after Frank passed away I found Huxley's book and it was an eye opener for me. When I read his description of Prayer of Adoration as "...the use of intellect, feeling, will and imagination in making acts of devotion directed towards God. . ." I had to smile another 'thank you, my friend, to Frank.'

I have a couple more short essays on meditation that have been very helpful to me: one from Ram Dass, the other from the Dalai Lama, part of which I included at the start of this guide.

Ram Dass writes in *Journey of Awakening,*

"Concentration is the root skill in all meditation practices. The meditator must be able to keep the mind fixed on a specific task or object, and let distractions go by, no matter which technique is used. This skill is simple in definition, but takes great patience to develop in practice. To begin developing concentration you need simply pick some object, thought, or part of the body and fix your mind on it for a fixed length of time. When your mind wanders, return you focus gently but firmly to the object of your meditation. Once you develop even a little concentration---which happens after a relatively short period of meditation---you will find it enhances all other methods of spiritual practice."(58)

He also writes,

"Try these directions for mindfulness of breathing, as a basic concentration practice. When you're ready to meditate, close your eyes and bring your attention to the motion of your breath as it enters and leaves your nostrils. Keep your focus at the nostrils, noting the full passage of each in-breath, from beginning to end. Don't follow the breath into your lungs or out into the air; just watch the flow in and out of your nostrils. If you can, notice the subtle sensations of the breath as it comes and goes.

Be aware of each in-breath and out-breath as it passes by the nostrils . . . Attend to the feeling of the breath. Don't try to imagine it or visualize it. Note the sensation of the breath just as it is, exactly as you feel it." . . . "Whenever you realize you're thinking about something else, return your awareness to your breath. Don't try to fight off thought. Just let them go." . . . "If sounds distract you do the same. Let them be and simply start watching your breath again. If aches or itches bother you, slowly move or shift to ease them if you must. But keep your mind on breathing while you do so." . . . Your mind will wander, and when you first start to meditate you may be acutely aware of how active it is. Don't worry about it. Just keep returning your attention to your breath, letting go of whatever the mind wanders to. This is the essence of meditation: Letting go of thoughts." (49-50)

I also took mantra suggestions from Ram Dass and at different times, I started on October 1 or April 1 and meditated on different mantras for 30 minutes a day for the next six months. These mantras included *Aum Mani Padme Hum*; *Ram-Ram, Ram-Ram*; *Gate Gate Paragate, Parasamgate, Bodhi Svaha*; and also, for two separate 6 month periods I followed his directions for mindfulness of breathing. As I mentioned earlier, during the period from 1 October, 1974 through 1 July, 2002 I did not miss a single day of at least 30 minutes of meditation every day. There were many others but those listed were my favorites.

The payoff for practicing my daily meditation has been a *gradual* reduction in my life long feelings of low-grade alert that something bad was about to happen; (the feeling of impending calamity described in the Big Book). This reduced level of anxiety gradually became the bedrock from which, coupled with working all the Steps in order, first each Step from the Big Book and then through the 12 and 12, enabled me to see that the living answer that Chuck C. talked about was built on the practice of basing my sense of well-being on "wanting what I was getting" rather than on "getting what I wanted."

Hello Dalai

In his book *"The Open Heart"* the Dalai Lama writes, "There are two methods of meditating that are to be used in our practice. One, analytical meditation, is the means by which we familiarize ourselves with the new ideas and mental attitudes. The other, settled meditation focuses the mind on a chosen subject." He also writes,

> "Although we all naturally aspire to be happy and wish to overcome our misery, we continue to experience pain and suffering. Why is this? . . . In our normal way of life, we let ourselves be controlled by powerful thoughts and emotions, which in turn give rise to negative states of mind. It is by this vicious circle that we perpetuate not only our unhappiness but also that of others. We must deliberately take a stand to reverse these tendencies and replace them with new habits. . . . We must nurture new inclinations by deliberately cultivating virtuous

practices. This is the true meaning and object of the practice of meditation."

"Familiarizing ourselves with the different aspect of our spiritual practice is therefore a form of meditation. Simply reading about them once is not of much benefit. If you are interested, it is helpful to contemplate the subjects mentioned . . . and then research them more extensively to broaden your understanding. The more you explore a topic and subject it to mental scrutiny, the more profoundly you understand it. This enables you to judge its validity. If through your analysis you prove something to be true, then your faith in that truth has powerful solidity. This whole process of research and scrutiny should be thought of as one form of meditation."

"As I have said, there are two types of meditation to be used in contemplating and internalizing the subjects I discuss in this book. First, there is analytical meditation. In this form of meditation, familiarity with a chosen object . . . is cultivated through the rational means of such analysis. . . . once you have developed familiarity with a topic by means of such analysis, it is important to remain focused on it by means of settled meditation in order to help it sink in more profoundly. . . . This occurs when we settle our minds on a chosen object without engaging in analysis or thought. . . . When we sense that our (consciousness of our chosen object) is weakening, we can again engage in analytical meditation to revitalize (our consciousness) before returning to settled meditation." . . . As we become more adept, we can skillfully switch between the two forms of meditation in order to intensify the desired quality."

In my experience, the Dalai Lama's combined Analytical-Settled meditation is similar to the meditation Bill W. described in his essay on Step 11 in the 12 and 12. This combined process has been the most effective for me in actually experiencing the pervasive presence and power of the Spirit of the Universe in my life.

For example, when we analyze our breathing process as it is providing oxygen to our circulatory system and nutrients to our cellular system, then transforming the oxygen to carbon dioxide and releasing that into the air through our out breath; coupled with plants circulating the carbon dioxide to give all the plant cells new life and converting the carbon dioxide back into oxygen for the plants to release oxygen back into the air for a later in breath for animal life. This analysis coupled with the analysis of the perfect distribution of particles and perfect balance in the forces of nature, resulting in gravity being the force of attraction that holds all massive bodies together so that the universe is made up as a single significant whole; coupled with the principled interaction of light from all over the entire universe with the principles of physics, biology and chemistry in our visual processes so we can see light with the naked eye from over 2 million light years away (Andromeda). These analyses and many others provide convincing evidence to me of the pervasive presence and power of the Spirit of the Universe underlying the "totality of things" manifesting order, harmony and goodness in every aspect of all being. Being conscious of that

My Life on a Frozen Lake

truth I am then able to "settle' into that presence and power. When our consciousness diminishes we can bring it back with the mantra: "The Spirit of God is within me;"" The Spirit of God surrounds me." Those mantras enable me to once again settle into the pervasive presence and power of the Spirit of the Universe.

About ten years ago Pat and I visited Egypt and throughout each day we experienced the call to prayer every two hours. Although I seldom actually do this I am committed to myself to add the slowed version of the Third Step Prayer, which I have included several times in this guide, to my meditation as I go through the day. However, because our culture goes full speed ahead all day every day it is more difficult than you might think to disengage from that to re-connect with your Higher Power. I remain committed to doing that anyway.

I have had countless experiences as a byproduct of the Steps, prayer and meditation where I have either received insight from my intellect on some issue after my brain was calmed by meditation and prayer; or, I have received guidance from a Spirit of the Universe underlying the totality of things. I am generally not sure about the source of guidance. When I first began having these experiences I was certain these insights were coming to me from my quieted brain. As time goes by I have a growing conviction that everything is guided by a Spirit of the Universe having All Powerful, Guiding, Creative Intelligence. In every instance, however, it comes to me as thoughts perhaps spoken by a voice. Examples of these experiences are included throughout this Guide and a few are italicized below.

In my first year, when I was working my way through the Steps from the Big Book, after I had listed all of my resentments of my dad from when I was a kid, I read the 'sick man's prayer' on pages 66 and 67 of the Big Book. I read it, open to the deeper meaning of each idea and phrase, but not as a prayer. That reading was immediately followed by my seeing my dad's behavior from an entirely different angle. I saw him as an alcoholic, who like me, based his sense of well-being on his having his way. His kids had to obey him, and for whatever reasons I was not behaving satisfactorily. He was convinced that part of his own behavior problems was that his parents had failed to discipline him and he was not going to make that mistake with me. That he had a seventh grade education and that he would not understand the concept of "trauma" if he heard it; that he would have believed that if I had trauma he could whip that out of me. Seeing my dad from that point of view I cut him lots of slack for the way he treated me. I saw that he was actually doing the best he could at that time. That before he passed on he joined AA and had several years sobriety when he died sober of a heart attack at an AA meeting. Years of resentment were almost immediately taken away. Up to then, in my mind, my dad was the blame for all my problems; after that all of my resentments of him were forgiven.

After I had gone through the Steps with George C., I was given an important assignment on the initial Proposal to the Army on a new Attack Helicopter that eventually came to be the Apache, AH 64. This was a very stressful assignment for me and I decided that my life was always going to be filled with stress; that life was never going to be worth living. I also knew that it would only get worse if I drank.

Without mentioning it to any one I decided that I was going to commit suicide. I had been studying USAARL 73-1 "Human Head and Neck Response to Impact Acceleration," as a requirement for crew station design. I decided to 'have an accidental Impact Acceleration' experience by driving my car into some roadside object. I had not mentioned this to anyone and I was not leaving any evidence of this being anything other than an accident. My company life insurance would pay my family double indemnity on my accidental death. *One evening, after another very stressful day, I was driving north on the Pacific Coast Highway on my way to a meeting in Malibu. I saw a semitrailer bed parked on the other side of the Highway without its tractor. I proceeded to the next opportunity to make a U-turn and then going south I was picking up speed to crash into the trailer. A thought, in the form of a voice, then came to me that said "It is alright with the Universe if you kill yourself; but the Universe doesn't know if you have fulfilled your purpose in life until you die. If you have killed yourself the Universe knows you did not fulfill your purpose and you have to start your existence over again from its beginning. The idea of starting life over again at its beginning was a horrible idea to me and I immediately abandoned the idea of suicide forever. I made another U-turn and went on to the AA meeting. Today I see this experience as another surrender, and as with drinking, the idea of suicide has been smashed.*

Meditative practices such as mantra and awareness of breathing in and out built a discipline that enables me to disengage from one line of thought and engage a better line of thought. In my breathing meditation I focus my attention on my breath coming in and going out. When my mind wanders to something else and I become aware of that I then return my focus to my breath. *As a result of the discipline, when Pat and I are arguing over some trifle and I become aware that my thinking is structuring my arguments I now have the discipline to disengage from the line of argument and engage the lyrics of the love song "But You Don't Know me," which is a great description of our relationship in High School which unfolded into our getting married on September 22, 1953. When I focus on those lyrics and the fact that she would finally fall in love with me too and we would be married, raise our children and find God together transform the argument into love.*

Short Story: As some of you know Pat over- decorates our home at Christmas time. The Christmas trees, Santa Clauses (3,000 of them) and all the decorations are stored in the garage attic. Sometime in September I climb into the attic and hand the decorations down to Pat for distribution throughout the house (inside and out). Throughout this process she instructs me on what she needs next; which I generally cannot find at that point in the procedure. Several years ago during this process she wanted a third Christmas tree handed down; I had already handed down two trees. I told her that "I do not see that tree, and if it is up here I'll eventually find it." She responded, "I know that it is up there. I distinctly remember handing it up to you last Christmas." I could have assured her that it was in the attic; that I simply could not reach it at that moment, but I decided not to.

She began to worry about the tree and from time to time she told me, "I know that tree is up there." Eventually I got to the tree and I handed it down to her. She was delighted not only that she had the tree but that she had been right in insisting it was in the attic. When, after a while, she called out to me "I knew that tree was up there and I was right." I waited a moment and then I responded: "Pat, honey, I just want you to know that I am getting sick of that Love Song." I didn't hear anything out of her for a few moments and then she climbed the ladder to put her head into the attic, and still laughing, said "You are not funny most of the time, but that was funny."

A major part of my job was to participate in periodic reviews of our technical, schedule and budgetary progress in the design of the Apache. The Army was also conducting similar reviews with Bell Helicopters, our competitor on the Apache Program, with the stress of 'competition' driving the design. I had continued with my meetings, meditations, sponsoring and service work but stress once again had built up in my work life and I decided I needed to get back into my previous work as a Tool Maker with some other company and with less stress. Pat agreed that I should find a less stressful job if the one I had made me feel like my life was not worth living. However, she asked me to find another job before I resigned my present one. When she told me that the stress immediately dissipated and I felt like the weight of the world was finally off my back. The next morning when I parked my car in my name stall I knew I was going to give up that parking place but that kind of stuff would not make any difference.

When I was a few steps from my office, the thought came to me as from a voice, "You are feeling really good this morning, aren't you Howard?" My response was the thought: "Yes I certainly am." "And," the thought/voice continued, "You have the same job this morning that you had yesterday but the stress is gone. Perhaps the stress was not from your job at all, but it was only your thinking." I went into my office, closed the door and set at my desk for a while contemplating that experience. I decided to dismiss the idea of changing jobs unless the stress returned to an unacceptable level again. Today I believe that is an example of spiritual progress manifest by a "Perfect Ideal" as described in Step 7 of the 12 X 12.

Early in my 13th year of sobriety I received a 15 % merit pay increase. I felt very disappointed because I had expected the increase to come with a promotion To Technical Section Manager. *During my meditation I experienced the pain of this disappointment and the thought, in the form of the voice, came to me: "The pain you are feeling has only one source: You want something that you do not believe you are going to receive. You are causing your own pain." That thought immediately freed me from the disappointment and from many others in the future.*

Within five weeks of the foregoing experience I received the promotion to Technical Section Manager with an additional 15 % pay increase as part of a reorganization of the Helicopter Design Division. In subsequent meditations I realized that these "coincidences" might be the manifestation of an All-Powerful, Guiding, Creative Intelligence underlying the totality of things. As Bill W. promised on page 46 of the

Big Book "We found that as soon as we were able to lay aside prejudice and express even a willingness to believe in a Power greater than ourselves, (that is: surrender) we commenced to get results, even though it was impossible for any of us to fully define or comprehend that Power, which is God."

The position of Technical Section Manager was my career goal and a "Baby Elephant Belief" I didn't realize I had was that it was stressful to work your way up to your career goal, but once you had reached your goal the stressful part of life would be over. Two days after I received the promotion my boss gave me an assignment to make a presentation to a 2 star general who was the Army's Program Manager on the Apache Helicopter. This presentation was a status report on the technical, schedule and budgetary position of the Fault Detection and Location System (FD/LS) for the first production helicopter. The General, his Technical Staff and three Ph.D. Physicists from John Hopkins University who were expert in these systems would attend the presentation and advise the General if FD/LS would be adequately developed to justify a recommendation to go into Production. I did not believe I was qualified to make this presentation and my boss felt like my recent promotion required me to make it.

The first few minutes of my meditation the next morning was simply experiencing the dread of risking my entire career in my first assignment as a Section Manager, and failing and never recovering from the failure. Then I was able to disengage from that stressful thought process and engage in my meditation. When my timer went off I felt relaxed and felt a sense of well-being. I didn't back out of my meditation, however, because I knew I would back out into the dreadfulness of that assignment. I then asked "Why do I have to med-itate in order to function. My boss doesn't meditate, his boss doesn't meditate. Why me?" Then, as if an answer to those questions in my mind's eye I saw a frozen lake. I knew that the ice on this lake was as thick as the laws of physics will allow ice to get. I knew that you could put a Sherman Tank on that ice and it would be supported. Then the thought, as if spoken by the voice, came to me: "Walking across the frozen lake a step at a time would be a good metaphor for living your life a 'day at a time' be careful because it is slippery." Then after a brief pause, "And by the way, Howard, if you are not convinced that the ice is thick enough to support you, you will dread every step you take." I was immediately convinced that this was Divine Guidance and that I could trust that this presentation would have Divine support. I did not mention this to my sponsor or anyone else. I believed it and did not want to risk losing the conviction by discussing it with anyone. The presentation was very successful and my convic-tion of the pervasive presence and power of Divine Order has remained as the hub of my life. (Divine Order is the pervasive presence of all the Power and Intelligence necessary to ensure the best possible outcome of every circumstance and event.)

Soon after the "Frozen Lake" meditation described above I was scheduled to make a technical presentation at the American Helicopter Society in Washington, D.C. Pat went to D.C. with me and while sightseeing in the nation's capital we visited the Holocaust Museum. The horror of the holo-caust was clearly displayed. In a video the museum showed an elderly survivor who told the story of how "We prayed and prayed that it would stop; but it went on and on. What good is Prayer?" the old survivor asked. When we left the museum my old doubts about prayer began to return. However, as I noted earlier my meditation practice followed the Big book guidance that when I was agitated or doubtful I should meditate about it.

Early that evening in our hotel room I got centered and restated the old survivor's question: "What good is prayer?" Very quickly I was fantasizing myself as being a hydrogen atom in the center of a star asking "How can there be a holocaust of hydrogen in a star created by a God who is both all-powerful and all good?" Very soon after I asked that question I saw the fusion process from an entirely different angle. The hydrogen atoms are fused into helium atoms; the helium atoms are later fused into carbon atoms; and later about half of the carbon atoms are fused into oxygen. In that way the elements required for the subsequent formation of life are being created by this stellar process. There is no loss of energy or matter; it is only changing form. Subsequent contemplation of this revealed to me that Divine Order is pervasive and is defined as all of the power and intelligence necessary to ensure the best possible outcome of every circumstance and event. Then later, all suffering is the essential beginning of some greater goodness that can only happen in this mystical way.

When I was 13 years sober and was going through the Steps again I worked the First Step from the directions in the Big Book and then in the 12 and 12 for a deeper and broader experience of the First Step. *When in an evening meditation I expressed doubt that I was personally powerless (as argued by Bill W. in the 12 X 12) because I had the power of choice and the power to perform tasks such as picking up a Big Book (which was on my lap at the time) with my hands. The thought then came to me, once again as if spoken by a voice, that whatever power I had, I had not given to myself. That all the power anyone has came from some other source of power. As I meditated on this over a series of evenings the truth that my entire being came from a Higher Power became clear to me. These meditations also convinced me that the similarity between individuals convincingly argued that all the power within each individual came from the same source of power. This gave the words a "Spirit of the Universe underlying the totality of things, having All-Powerful, Guiding, Creative Intelligence" a totally new meaning to me.*

Coming to believe in the pervasive presence and power of God underlying everything completely revised the Twelve Steps for me. For example, before I was on "the basis of trusting and relying upon God . . . " and was totally self-reliant my review of my Fears revealed "an evil and corroding thread; the fabric of my existence was shot through with it. . . ." The primary results of these self-reliant reviews were that most of the things I feared would happen didn't happen. When I believed in the presence of God in my life I could credit God with the fact that these things did not happen. In addition, when I considered my fear of not getting employment as a civilian electrician and my fear that I would be laid off as a tool maker, and the things I feared would happen did happen, the thought came to me, as if from a spoken voice, that not taking either of those career paths was the best thing that could have happened. As an Electrician Mate in the Navy I had learned everything I needed to learn about engineering design requirements for weapon systems to be maintained by a 17 year old kid with a high school education and little maintenance training. As a tool maker I learned Engineering tolerances, manufacturing tolerances, manufacturing process capabilities, and other requirements necessary to perform well as an Engineering Design Manager. When ". . . I trust infinite God rather than my finite self. . . ." I see God pulling a golden thread though every circumstance and event in my life, which I could not see in my finite self because I was not having my way.

The Program has transformed me in ways that could not have happened outside the program. Every change I have been able to experience for the better has come to me through all the 12 steps and the spiritual insights I have experienced have all been connected to Prayer and Meditation. Intellectual analyses (having things make sense to me) have been essential to my growth. However, intellect and logic does not directly improve my conscious contact with God. That requires prayer and meditation and conscious participation with God in my life.

Appendix III includes a list of books and other sources that have been helpful to me in understanding alcoholism/drug addiction and finding God and my life in our universe. One of the books included is entitled *"Why God Won't Go Away"* which provides an overview of the pioneering work that Andrew Newberg, M.D. and the late Eugene D'Aquili, M. D., Ph.D., have done in neural scientific studies of the relationship between spirituality and the central nervous system. In part their studies identified shifts in neurological activities experienced by Tibetan Monks and Franciscan Nuns while they were meditating.

As described by Jill Bolte Taylor, Ph.D. former Professor of Brain Anatomy at Harvard Medical School and author of the book, *"My Stroke of Insight"* there was a reduction of activity in the left hemisphere language centers which silenced their brain chatter. Coupled with that, there was a decrease in activity in the orientation association area. When the neural activities in these areas of the brain occur, the individuals experience a shift in consciousness from being an individual to that of feeling at one with the universe.

As a Deist, I did not believe that the insights I experienced in meditation were spiritual insights. I believed that these insights came to me from my intellect after my "brain chatter" had been reduced by disengaging from the fight-or-flight center of the brain through meditation.

> Another Short Story: Clancy and I were participating in an AA History Conference. I told the story about meditating on "my admission of personal powerless,' from the essay on the First Step in the 12 X 12. I described my experience as ". . . a voice said to me, give yourself the power to levitate the Big Book." After my share Clancy said to me, "Howard, you gave a very good history talk on Bill writing the 12 and 12. Your research was excellent as was your topic. (I suspect he appreciated that my topic did not walk over his topics). But I want to explain two things to you: When we talk to God we call that Prayer. When God talks to us we call that Schizophrenia."

That is a funny line which I now repeat frequently, but as I mentioned earlier, I am not always sure where the insight comes from. Gradually I have stopped worrying about that because if the Spirit underlies the totality of things then it underlies my every thought and experience if I am conscious of it or not. I have come to see that my intellect and logic are not the answer here. Prayer and meditation and my love of my life and everything in it are the contact points.

In retrospect, my spiritual growth has been slow and unsteady, but clearly, for me "Constructive Meditation (and prayer) is a primary requirement of every step in my spiritual growth."

Step Twelve

§

"Having had a spiritual awakening as the result of
these steps, we tried to carry this message to alcoholics,
and to practice these principles in all our affairs."

HAVING A SPIRITUAL AWAKENING AS *THE* result of these steps is
an impressive goal and promise for us and to us. In Appendix
II in The Big Book, Bill W. wrote: "He finally realizes that he
has undergone a profound alteration in his reaction to life; that
such a change could hardly have been brought about by himself
alone. What often takes place in a few months could seldom
have been accomplished by years of self-discipline. With few
exceptions our members find that they have tapped an unsuspected inner resource *which they presently identify with their own*
conception of a Power greater than themselves. . . . Most of us think the
awareness of a Power greater than ourselves is the essence of spiritual
experience. Our more religious members call it "God-consciousness."
(My italics)

The transformation from a seemingly hopeless state of
mind and body to a sober human being conscious of the
presence of, and their connection with, an unsuspected inner

spiritual resource is *THE* result of alcoholics working the Twelve Steps of Recovery. Amazing, yet, as my sponsor, Bob B., emphasizes: "No one among us, regardless how intelligent he is, how hard he works at it, or how long he has been sober has come close to getting all the goodness that is available from working these Twelve Steps and the other spiritual practices in the AA Program. There is just too much available through these practices." Hopefully, if you have worked the Steps at all you have begun to have this experience even though you may not have identified that that is what has happened.

Chapter 7 in the Big Book "Working with Others," describes in great detail how we carry the message to others. This description of Twelfth Step work is both thorough and profound and I encourage everyone to study this Chapter which addresses most courses of action that we will encounter in our efforts to carry the message. I am not going to make any effort to excerpt passages out of that Chapter for use in the guide.

Bill also did a thorough and profound job of summarizing the spiritual awakening that comes to us as a result of working the Twelve Steps in his essay on Step Twelve in the 12X12. My effort in this guide to the Twelfth Step will be limited to suggesting that you carefully read Chapter 7 "Working with Others" in the Big Book; and Step Twelve in the 12 and 12. I am going to limit my comments on Step Twelve to discussing some of the principles underlying the 12 Steps and to summarizing some information describing that GOD is in fact the underlying principle in the Steps and in everything that exists in the Universe.

PRACTICE WHAT PRINCIPLES IN ALL OUR AFFAIRS?

Many of us have asked the question, "What are the principles we are to practice in all our affairs?"

While I am sure that the 12 descriptive words listed on many Alano Club walls are important attributes to practice in our recovery, I have never believed that they accurately summarize the Principles in each of the Steps with which they are listed. Neither do I believe that this guide is going to fully answer that question. I am hopeful that by making this effort we can have a clearer understanding of how they interact in our lives as we work the Steps.

The single word Principles frequently used to describe the "principle" involved in each Step are:

Step One: Honesty
Step Two: Hope
Step Three: Faith
Step Four: Courage
Step Five: Integrity
Step Six: Willingness
Step Seven: Humility
Step Eight: Brotherly Love
Step Nine: Discipline
Step Ten: Perseverance
Step Eleven: Spiritual Awareness
Step Twelve: Service

Undoubtedly these 12 spiritual attributes are important to the working of *each* step. However, Bill W. has written at the start of Step Seven in the 12 and 12; Greater humility is the bedrock on which each of AA's Twelve Steps are built. It also appears to me that honesty, hope, faith, courage and most of the others are essential attributes needed in all of the Twelve Steps.

While acknowledging once again that this guide will probably not answer the question proposed about 'what are the principles that we practice?' I want to explain my approach to finding an answer. I first indexed the word **principles** in the Big Book and studied their usages in each context in which the word was used. The specific sentences using the words and the page numbers in the Big Book which they are found are listed below:

My friend had emphasized the absolute necessity of demonstrating these *principles* in all our affairs. p14

A much more important demonstration of our *principles* lies before us in our respective homes, occupations and affairs. p19

Quite as important was the discovery that spiritual *principles* would solve all my problems. P42

That was great news for us, for we had assumed we could not make use of spiritual *principles* unless we accepted many things on faith which seemed difficult to believe. P47

Having had a spiritual awakening as the result of these steps, we tried to carry this message to alcoholics, and to practice these *principles* in all our affairs. p60

No one among us has been able to maintain anything like perfect adherence to these *principles*. p60

The *principles* we have set down are guides to progress. p60

Although these reparations take innumerable forms, there are some general *principles* which we find guiding. p79

The main thing is that he be willing to believe in a Power greater than himself and that he live by spiritual *principles*. p93

We are dealing with only general *principles* common to most denominations. p 94

In nearly every instance these uses of the word principles were in the context of working the Steps or the result of working the Steps. The Steps themselves imply that following the principles of the Steps in their specified sequence will result in our being transformed from a life of self-centeredness to a life of practicing Spiritual Principles in all of our affairs; and having an ongoing conscious awareness of the presence and power of the Spirit of the Universe in our lives.

Now looking into my Webster's I find:

"Principle" (1) The laws or facts of nature underlying the working of an artificial device; (2) A distinguishing ingredient that exhibits or imparts a characteristic

quality; (3) A comprehensive and fundamental law, doctrine, or assumption; (4) a rule or code of conduct; (5)
Christian Science: a divine principle: GOD.

"Spirit:" (1) Incorporeal or immaterial being

"Spiritual:" (1) of, relating to, or consisting of spirit.

Although I intend to further research the "spiritual" nature of
principles in the writings of others, I would like to review some
of the actions we take in working the Steps and see if there are
Scientific or Spiritual Principles underlying them, and if so,
what are they.

When alcoholics drink so much that they destroy their lives,
they are defying their desire for self-preservation. When they
are humbled to this level of "surrendering to win" the Spirit of
God can enter and smash the delusion that they can drink like
normal people. While it is only with Step One that they experience 100% success, the remaining Steps state perfect goals; and
serve as a yardstick by which they measure their progress in the
remaining Eleven Steps. Thus, 'surrender to win' becomes a
principle practiced in all Twelve Steps.

This description reflects closely what Bill first learned in his
visit to Townes Hospital where he had his last drink. On page
64 of "Alcoholics Anonymous Comes of Age," he notes that
Ebby, brought him a copy of William James' *Variety of Religious
Experience*. Admitting that it was a hard read, Bill read it from
cover to cover while still in the hospital. In so doing, he saw that
each Spiritual Experience described in James' book included

the individual being completely defeated in some important area of his life, admitting that he was defeated, knowing he needed help, and asking for that help.

Now, looking at each subsequent increment in each of following eleven Steps, when I see how this "principle" applies: The depth of my surrender to the fact that I lack the power to wrest satisfaction and happiness out of this world by my managing well; the clarity and conviction with which I come to believe that my creator is my partner in this entire business of living before I reach a level of humility that I can decide to turn my will and my life over to His care. Then, for this decision to have a lasting effect, I must experience deflation at depth from my inability to practice acceptance and forgiveness instead of anger and resentment when I do not have my way. When I see the depth of my selfishness in not having one relationship where I am not in it to take from it and that without help I cannot change; that I cannot practice rigorous honesty without help; that I cannot stop seeking positions of authority for prestige and the like; that I can't practice Faith instead of Fear without relying on infinite God rather than my finite self; and then that I must rely on God to keep me from seeking gratification from life through all the other short term pleasures that do not address my long term problem of selfishness and self-centeredness. And so on through the Steps.

In every Step we must experience 'utter defeat,' 'be utterly desperate,' and to make 'an appeal for help.' This is certainly consistent with Bill's insistence on page 70 of the 12 X 12: that the attainment of more humility is the bedrock principle of each of AA's Twelve Steps.

In a similar way, I find that each of the "single word principles" identified with each Step are all applicable to every Step. Honesty, Hope, Faith, Courage, Integrity, Willingness, Brotherly Love, Discipline, Perseverance, Spiritual Awareness, Service with Humility are foundation principles of every Step.

In addition, these are at least some of the same principles that we are to practice in all our affairs.

Now, because the Dictionary included a definition of 'principle' as: "Christian Science: a divine principle: GOD," I looked up the word Principle in *"Science and Health with Key to the Scriptures,"* by Mary Baker Eddy, the founder of the Christian Science Religion. In the Glossary, PRINCIPLE was referred to recapitulation, on Page 465, in the Question and Answer Section, which stated:

"Question--- Is there more than one God or Principle?

Answer --- There is not.

Principle and its idea is one, and this one is God, omnipotent, omniscient, and Omni-Present Being, and His reflection is man and the universe. . . . Hence God combines all-power or potency, all-science or true knowledge, all-presence. The varied manifestations of Christian Science indicate Mind, never matter, and have one Principle."

Mary Baker Eddy's spiritual viewpoints may have been too extreme in assuming that every person could practice God's presence in their life to ensure good health. But her viewpoints were among the first "New Age" ideas about spirituality. The idea that God is in Himself the principle that combines all principles: All Power, all-science, all presence. As indicated by the following quotations, other spiritual teachers of that period agree.

Next, I indexed the word principles in H. Emilie Cady's little book "*Lessons in Truth*," which was copy written in 1894 and revised in1953, and was published by Unity School of Christianity. I selected passages from those indexed pages which I thought might be applicable to defining the principles or principle described in the Big Book. Those passages are included below:

"Many have thought of God as a personal being. The statement that God is Principle chills them, and in terror they cry out, 'They have taken away my Lord, and I know not where they have laid him.' (John 20:13) Broader and more learned minds are always cramped by the thought of God as a person, for personality limits to place and time."

"God is the name we give to that unchangeable, inexorable principle at the source of all existence. To the individual consciousness God takes on all things. He is principle, impersonal as expressed in each individual. He becomes personal to that one—a personal, loving, all-forgiving Father-Mother. All that we can ever need or desire is the infinite Father-Principle, the great reservoir of unexpressed good. There is no limit to the Source of our being, nor to His willingness to manifest more of Himself through us, when we are willing to do His will."

"Hitherto we have turned our hearts and efforts toward the external for fulfillment of our desires and for satisfaction, and we have been grievously disappointed. For the hunger of everyone for satisfaction is only the cry of the homesick child for its Father-Mother God. It is only the Spirit's desire in us to come forth into our consciousness as more and more perfection, until we shall have become fully conscious of our oneness with All-perfection. Man never has been, never can be satisfied with anything less." (Pages 22-23)

"There is no real reason why we, having come to recognize God as infinite substance, should be by this recognition deprived of the familiar fatherly companionship that in all ages has been so dear to the human heart. There is no necessity for us to separate God as substance and God as tender Father; no reason why we should not, and every reason why we should, have both in one; they are one—God principle outside of us as unchangeable law, God within us as tender, loving Father-Mother, who has compassion for our every sorrow."

"There is no reason why, because in our earlier years some of us were forced into the narrow puritanical limits that stood for a religious belief, we should now so exaggerate our freedom as to fancy that we are entirely self-sufficient and shall never again need the sweet, uplifting communion between Father and child. The created, whoever lives, moves, and has his being in his Creator, needs the conscious presence of that Creator, and cannot be entirely happy in knowing God only as cold, unsympathetic Principle. Why cannot both conceptions find lodgment in the minds and hearts? Both are true, and both are necessary parts of a whole. The two were made to go together, and in the highest cannot be separated." (Pages 136-137).

Next I indexed the word principle in Earnest Holmes book "*The Science of Mind*," copy written in 1938. I selected Earnest Holmes because he was the founder of the Church of Religious Science, and he was Chuck C.'s teacher, friend (and sponsor?) and because his book contains clearly stated (and re-stated) spiritual principles to be practiced in all of our affairs concurrent with the general period when Bill W. wrote the Big Book.

"THE PRINCIPLE RE-STATED: Let us restate our Principle. We are surrounded by an Infinite Possibility. It is Goodness, Life, Law and Reason. In expressing itself through us, it becomes more fully conscious of its own being. Therefore, it wishes to express itself through us. As It passes into our being, It automatically becomes the law of our lives. It can pass into expression through us only as we consciously allow it to do so. Therefore, we should have faith in it, and its desires and its ability to do for us *all that we shall ever need to have done*. Since it must pass through our consciousness to operate for us, we must be conscious that it is doing so." (Page 46)

"PLACE NO LIMIT ON PRINCIPLE: Know your own mind. Train yourself to think what you wish to think; be what you wish to be; feel what you wish to feel, and place no limit on Principle! The words which you speak would be just as powerful as the words which Jesus spoke, if you knew your word was the law whereunto it was sent, but you must KNOW this WITHIN and not merely accept it with your intellect. If you have reached a point where the inner consciousness believes, then your word is simply an announcement of Reality! KNOW-without a shadow of doubt---that as a result of your treatment, some action takes place in infinite Mind. If you have a vague, subtle, unconscious fear, be quite and ask yourself, "Who am I?" "What am I?" "Who is speaking?" "What is my life?" In this manner think right back to Principle, until your thought becomes perfectly clear again. Such is the power of right thinking, that it cancels and erases everything unlike itself. It answers every question, solves all problems, is the solution to every difficulty. It is like the sunlight of Eternal Truth, bursting through the clouds of obscurity and bathing all life in glory. It is the Absolute with which you are dealing. ALL THERE REALLY IS IS GOD." (Page 188)

The foregoing information is far from comprehensive, but I think it is a fair representation of the understanding, ideas and attitudes that might have influenced Bill W. when he was working on the Big Book and the Twelve Steps. As noted earlier I am inclined to think that Bill W. has included any and all of the dictionary definitions of "spiritual principles" and "Principle Being" in the Steps; and that we can identify them from the context in which they were used.

However, common sense tells me that we only have two forms in which something can exist: Material or Spiritual. Common Sense also tells me that if something is going to freely integrate with all forms of material then the form of that integrating thing would have to be non-material or Spiritual. Further, if intelligence and power are integrated with all material being they must be spiritual in nature. This leads me to believe that there is a single spirit in all material being and that it manifests principle, intelligence and power; as well as forgiveness, compassion and perfect love of all that exists. Therefore, " . . . the perfectly logical assumption (principle) is that underneath the material world and life as we see it, there is an All Powerful, Guiding, Creative Intelligence." Page 49, Big Book

Whats the Point?

§

IN CLOSING, I WANT TO review some 'highlights' that I first gleaned from Chuck C. from 1972 when I first heard him speak until very recently when I was listening to some old cd's of his talks. Throughout my time in the program most of the "baby elephant" spiritual beliefs I brought into the Program with me have been gradually replaced by things I heard Chuck share and came to know through the 12 Steps. Although I have put them in quotes, they are essentially from memory and are not necessarily *verbatim*.

"There is only one problem in this life, which includes all problems. Fortunately, there is one answer that includes all answers. The one problem is a conscious feeling of separation from . . . from what? From Life, Good, God . . . three words that are synonymous to me. That, I believe, is the best definition of the human ego that you will ever find. While that feeling of separation is a real feeling, it is not reality. Because nothing can exist apart from, if it exists it exists as a part of. The Living answer then to every Living problem is a conscious feeling of Unity with Life, Good, God. "

"The ancients tell us that on one hand there is the Law; and on the other hand there is Love. The Law is: Whatever you sew that you shall reap. You cannot plant carrots and get radishes. You put slop in; you are going to get slop back. Love is the fulfillment of the Law. If you put Love in you can only get Love back."

"It's my opinion that there isn't a Living Answer, for the non-alcoholic or the alcoholic alike that does not include a personally satisfactory, conscious partnership with the God that made us in this entire business of living."

The last time I heard Chuck share before he passed on in 1984 was at the Martyr's Meeting in Redondo Beach, California. It may have been a Saturday night or a Sunday morning. His mind was clearer than it had been the last few times I had heard him share. As I remember he told us:

"I want to share with you something I saw from the picture window in my living room. First, I saw a blue jay fly into my yard. After watching the blue jay for a while it was joined by a hummingbird. Now there is a bird that can show you some 'di-does:' it flies straight up and down, sideways, backwards, and hovers in one spot. I watched both birds for a while and I then had the thought: 'if I was a blue jay I would want to be a hummingbird. But the blue jay doesn't want to be a hummingbird, it wants to be a blue jay, and *it knows how*.' . . . Next I want to share about the salmon that is born in the mouth of the Klamath River. It joins with a large school of other salmon and swims the entire round trip to the Sea of Japan and back to the mouth of the Klamath River to the exact spot where it was born, to spawn and to die. . . . Then, there is the swallow that flies into Capistrano, a coast town near my home in Laguna Beach. Every year, on this same day, the swallows arrive in Capistrano from their long flight from South America. Isn't that something? . . . Now, boys and girls, what is the point I am trying to make here? My point is: If God would give a blue jay, a hummingbird, a salmon and a swallow everything they need to fulfill their destiny? Would He do less for you?"

In conclusion, it is also clear to me that these changes could have only happened for me through the Twelve Steps of Recovery.

APPENDIX I

Science Tells Us So. We Have No Reason To Doubt It

§

Dr. Richard Feynman, winner of the Nobel Prize for Physics in 1965, in the first volume of his three volume set of *"Lectures on Physics,"* wrote: "It is important to realize that in Physics today, we have no knowledge of what energy is. We do not have a picture that energy comes in little blobs of a definite amount. It is not that way. . . . It is an abstract thing in that it does not tell us the mechanism or the reasons for the various formulas." Vol. 1, page 4-2)

Dr. Einstein wrote: "Everyone who is seriously involved in the pursuit of science becomes convinced that a spirit is manifest in the laws of the Universe." Science tells us that Energy becomes material at the exchange rate of E=mc ^{2} Inasmuch as this "exchange rate" *is in accordance with this precise law of the Universe, science then suggests that it might well be the manifestation of an underlying Spirit.*

When we contemplate Dr. Feynman's comment on the mysteries of energy, coupled with Dr. Einstein's conviction that a spirit is manifest in all natural laws, then there is certainly room for rationally concluding that energy is in fact spirit/energy.

Science also tells us that following a brief inflationary era the Universe was a boiling caldron of quarks, gluons and leptons. Up Quarks have a positive 2/3rds electrical charge and Down Quarks have a negative 1/3rd electrical charge. Hence, when two Up Quarks bond with one Down Quark (bonded together by the strong force) a Proton is created having a +1 electrical charge. When two Down Quarks bond together with one Up Quark, a Neutron is created with a 0 electrical charge. The electron, a fundamental particle, has an inherent negative electrical charge of exactly -1. Thus far it has been impossible to distinguish any differences in the value of any of the electrical charges from one Proton to another, one Neutron to another or one Electron to another. This is very close tolerance work.

Science also tells us that, if the rate of expansion of the Universe after one second had been 1 part out of one hundred thousand million million parts slower than it was, gravity would have pulled the universe back in on itself before stars or galaxies could had formed. On the other hand, if it had been expanding one part in a million parts faster than it did, the expansion would have been too fast for the formation of stars and galaxies. This I see as another example of very close tolerance work.

Now, what about the strong, electro/magnetic, weak and gravitational forces? Science tells us that if we assign a value of 1 to gravity, then we must assign corresponding values of 10 to the 25th power to the weak force; 10 to the 37th power to the electro/magnetic force and 10 to the 39th power to the strong force. So how did gravity get to play such a dominating role in the expansion? The strong force bonds quarks together to form Protons and Neutrons and bonds Protons and Neutrons together to form atomic nuclei. Although the strong force is by far the strongest force its reach is very short, essentially bumper to bumper. With the electro/magnetic force, like charges repel and unlike charges attract. When a negative electron and its -1 electrical charge bonds through attraction to a +1 electrically charged proton, the negative and positive electric charges cancel each other exactly and the electric charge is neutralized, thus gravity becomes the dominating force (which always attracts directly proportional to the product of the masses and inversely proportional to the distance between the masses squared) of attraction that hold the universe's massive bodies together as a single significant whole.

To use Dr. Richard Feynman's language from Vol. II, Chapter 1 of his Lecture Notes on Physics, the distribution of particles and the balance of the forces of nature are perfect. Perfect is also an example of very close tolerance work.

From 200 to 500 million years after the Big Bang creation began, galaxy sized clouds of hydrogen and helium formed and concentrations of gravity within these clouds began to form them into the cores of stars made up of about 75 percent Hydrogen and 25 percent Helium. The formation of stars involve a two-step fusion process where gravitational pressure from outer layers of hydrogen and helium initially cause hydrogen nuclei in the core of the star to fuse into deuterium nuclei (1 proton, 1 neutron); then into tritium (2 protons, 1 neutron) and then into helium (2 protons and two neutrons). Because there are no stable nuclei made up of any combination of five protons and neutrons, the first step of the two step process is to continue to fuse hydrogen into helium until the necessary abundance of helium and thermal properties are achieved for the second step of the process to start.

The second step of the two step process is the fusion of helium into heavier nuclei, which takes place when the necessary abundance of helium is available as well as high enough thermal properties.

I am now going to turn to my favorite science writer, Timothy Ferris, and his book "The Whole Shebang." Ferris tells us that "Carbon is the fourth most abundant cosmic element, after hydrogen, helium and oxygen. It is also the basis of terrestrial life. (That's why the study of carbon compounds is known as *organic* chemistry.) Carbon atoms are made inside stars. To make one takes three helium nuclei. The trick is to get two helium nuclei to stick together until they are struck by a third. It turns out that this feat depends critically on the internal resonances of carbon and oxygen nuclei. . . . No carbon, no us, so our existence depends in some sense on the fine-tuning of these two nuclear resonances."

Now, Dr. Ferris turns to Doctor Fred Hoyle, a brilliant and sometimes atheistic astrophysicist -astronomer. He tells us that Hoyle declared that his atheism was shaken by his discovery of these finely tuned resonances. "If you wanted to produce carbon and oxygen in roughly equal quantities by stellar nucleosynthesis, these are just the two levels you have to fix, if your fixing would have to be just about where these levels are actually found to be. . . . Is that another put-up, artificial job? I am inclined to think so. A common sense interpretation of the facts suggests that a super intellect has monkeyed with physics, as well as with chemistry and biology, and that there are no blind forces worth speaking about in nature. The numbers one calculates from the facts seem to me so overwhelming as to put this conclusion almost beyond question."

Once started, this second step creates most of the elements in the Periodic Table, including carbon, oxygen, silicon and iron. Inasmuch as iron cannot be fused by this process without adding more energy, the gravitational pressures on the iron core eventually break the core and it collapses into the most energetic explosion known to science: a super nova. This explosion blasts the debris from the exploding star, and results in producing elements heavier than iron, including lead, gold, and on up to and including uranium, which are fused from the forces and temperatures of the explosion, out into stellar space. To me, the fact that this is a two-step process (actually three counting the super nova) that eventually resulted in a life breeding universe is convincing evidence of the presence of a creative intelligence, a Spirit of the Universe guiding the creative processes into producing that outcome.

In one specific primary star, the hydrogen and helium in its debris were gravitationally formed into a second generation star that we call the sun, and a ring of heavier elements was formed around the star. Gradually these heavier elements were accreted into the planets Mercury, Venus, Earth, Mars, a belt of meteorites, Jupiter, Saturn, Uranus and Neptune. The Earth is at the perfect distance from the sun to experience thermal properties necessary to establish an abundance of liquid water where organic matter could form and from which life ultimately came into being.

In 1953, when Pat and I were married, a chemist working on his PhD at the University of Chicago, named Stanley

Miller, conducted an experiment that spontaneously created organic chemicals that are essential to the existence of proteins and therefore to life. When I entered Wichita University in September, 1954, there was an article written by Dr. George Wald, a Harvard Biologist, in which he convincingly argued that during an estimated 2 billion year period, random variations in chemical makeup coupled with available energy sources, such as lightening, had combined to spontaneously create life on earth. At that time I was struggling to disengage from my earlier religious teachings so Dr. Wald's article, and Dr. Fred Hoyle's '*Steady State Theory*,' which had no beginning and therefore didn't need a creator, persuaded me to try to become an atheist. I soon changed into a Deist when I heard that that was what Dr. Einstein's religious belief was called.

Some 27 years later, when I was 9 years sober in the program, I gradually opened my mind to the possibility that God did indeed participate in our lives. It occurred to me to check on what had happened with my two scientific heroes who had persuaded me that there might not be a God in our world. I found an article in the Engineering Library at work where I first read about Dr. Hoyle's reaction to the discovery of the finely tuned resonances of Carbon and Oxygen mentioned above. Later I found that Dr. George Wald's famous article in Scientific American had been republished and at his request had been withdrawn. He had said that the article was wrong; that there had not been a 2 billion year period of random variations in which life could have formed, but that life came into being almost immediately when the thermal properties and abundances of liquid water were available to support life.

When Dr. Wald was asked, "If you no longer believe today what you believe in 1954, what do you believe now?" He replied: "Several years ago (when he was working on vision for which he was awarded a Nobel Prize in Biology) . . . a thought struck me that at first seemed so aberrant as to embarrass me." . . . "I and almost all other biologists have the thought that mind (is) a late product in evolution, dependent on the development of complex central nervous systems. . . . The aberrant thought had been one that I still have, and that is that 'mind . . . had been there from the start; and that this became that intrinsically very improbable thing, a life-breeding Universe because the constant and pervasive presence of mind had guided it into become that." (Dennis Brian, '*Genius Talk*,' page 146-47)

The last time slice of what I believe describes the pervasive intelligence and power of Divine Order is in a book entitled, *The Incredible Machine*, published by the National Geographic Society, which states:

"The newborn baby embodies innocence, yet conceals the most taunting of all riddles: the generation of human life. The story begins with sperm and egg as they combine to form a single cell. Sheltered in the mothers' womb, the cell multiplies. Soon there are hundreds of different cells able to make some 50,000 different proteins to control the work of all our cells---collagen to build skin, insulin to control energy use, hemoglobin to supply oxygen. Before long, the groups of cells are gathering into layers, then into sheets and tubes, sliding into the proper places at the proper times, forming an eye exactly where an eye should be, the pancreas where the pancreas belongs. The order of appearance is precise, with structures like veins and nerves appearing just in time to support the organs that will soon require them. In four weeks the progeny of the first cell have shaped a tiny beating heart; in only three months they are summoning reflex responses from a developing brain. Nothing more than specks of chemicals animate the nascent cells as they divide. Yet in just nine months, some twenty five trillion cells will emerge together from the womb; together they will jump and run and dance; sing, weep, imagine and dream." Page 13, *"The Incredible Machine"*

The perfectly reasonable assumption is that an order and harmony is manifest in physics, chemistry and biology which led to this becoming a life breeding universe; an order and harmony that provides convincing evidence that there is a Spirit of the Universe underlying the totality of things. The Spirit would have to manifest All-Powerful, Guiding, Creative Intelligence to sustain the creation from its start to where it is today, always transforming itself into indeterminate processes and parameters. It does not make sense(see page 93, Big Book) to believe that the Universe unfolded in order and harmony for 13.7 billion years without me being in it and that I then came into being in 1932 and took charge of my entire life and as much of yours and theirs as I could. Common sense, when it becomes uncommon sense, tells me that through the Grace of the Spirit I am a participant but that I am not in control of outcomes.

While I am speaking about "common sense becoming uncommon sense" I am going to point out some interesting similarities in some Spiritual quotations of Dr. Einstein and of Bill W. in the Big Book.

Dr. Einstein, *"The World as I See It"* page 5: "A knowledge of the existence of something we cannot penetrate, of the manifestations of the profoundest reason and most radiant beauty, which are only accessible to our reason in their most elementary forms---it is this knowledge and this emotion that constitute the truly religious attitude; in this sense, and in this alone, I am a deeply religious man."

Bill W., Big Book, page 46: "We found that as soon as we were able to lay aside prejudice and express even a willingness to believe in a Power greater than ourselves, we commenced to get results, even though it was impossible for any of us to fully define or comprehend that Power, which is God."

In Isaacson, *"Einstein"* Page 388 quotation: "Everyone who is seriously involved in the pursuit of science becomes convinced that a spirit is manifest in the laws of the Universe---a spirit vastly superior to that of man, and one in the face of which we with our modest powers must feel humble. In this way the pursuit of science leads to a religious feeling of a special sort."

Bill W. Big Book, Page 46: "As soon as we admitted the possible existence of a Creative Intelligence, A Spirit of the Universe underlying the totality of things, we began to be possessed of a new sense of power and direction, provided we took other simple steps."

Dr. Einstein, *"The World as I See It,"* Page 26: "But there is a state of religious experience which I will call cosmic religious feeling. The individual feels the nothingness of human desires and aims (Step One) and the sublimity and marvelous order which reveal themselves both in nature and the world of thought. (Step Two) He looks upon his individual existence as a sort of prison and wants to experience the universe as a single significant whole. (Step Three) . . . "How can cosmic religious feeling be communicated from one person to another, if it can give rise to no definite notion of a God and no theology? In my view, it is the most important function of art and science to awaken this feeling and keep it alive in those capable of it."

Bill W., Big Book, Page 49: "The prosaic steel girder is a mass of electrons whirling around each other at incredible speed. These tiny bodies are governed by precise laws. And these laws hold true throughout the material world. Science tells us so. We have no reason to doubt it.

Isaacson, *"Einstein"* Page 389: "I believe in Spinoza's God, who reveals himself in the lawful harmony of all that exists . . ."

Bill W., Big Book, Page 53: "We had to fearlessly face the proposition that God was everything or else He is nothing."

It might also be noted that the Science of Bill W.'s time and the Science of today has changed a great deal. During the 20th Century the "indeterminacy" of Quantum Physics has become a fundamental part of Science. Dr. Einstein, throughout his life in science was convinced that everything has been pre-determined, and that "God does not play dice with the Universe." Quantum Physics has proven that indeterminacy is a fundamental fact of science. Quoting Doctor Feynman, in his book titled *"QED,"* "The theory of quantum electrodynamics has lasted now for more than fifty years, and has been tested more and more accurately over a wider and wider range of conditions. At the present time I can proudly say that there is *no significant difference* between experiment and theory. . . . To give you a feeling for the accuracy of these numbers, it comes out something like this: If you were to measure the distance from Los Angeles to New York to this accuracy, it would be exact to the thickness of a human hair." (*QED*, page 7)

So what? So God "does shoot dice" with the universe. Okay, Okay, but So What? Well, if God designed and implemented quantum physics it would be a perfect dice game; and in a perfect dice game God Himself could not know what the next roll of the dice is going to be. He does know that it will not be less than a two nor more than a twelve, and that $1/6^{th}$ of the time it will be a seven and right on down the probability curve. So it is a tightly bound universe but the next roll of the dice is unknown even to God. Why? Because God wanted it that way. (Which I think is a good answer for all Why Questions).

In his book, "*The Faith of a Physicist,*" Dr. John Polkinghorne, discussed this issue on pages 150-151 as follows: "Pannenberg puts the issue squarely before us." "Contemporary theology lacks a doctrine of the Holy Spirit that corresponds in breadth to the biblical concept of the Spirit. Such a doctrine would require a treatment of our present knowledge of the causes of life. Can we still speak today of a 'spiritual' origin of all life? What sense would such talk have with respect to the phenomena and structures of life that have been explored by biology?"

Taylor's response would be that . . . "if we think of a Creator at all, we are to find him always on the inside of creation. And if God is really on the inside, we must find him in the processes, not in the gaps. We know now there are no gaps, no points at which a special intervention is conceivable. From first to last the process has been continuous. Nature is all of a piece, a seamless robe . . . If the hand of God is to be recognized in this continuous creation, it must be found not in isolated intrusions, . . . but in the very process itself."

To which Polkinghorne adds: "To reject the idea of a fitful divine interventionism is not to embrace the deistic notion of a self-contained universe left to the unfolding of its inevitable history. The concept of divine interaction within cosmic process, through the input of information into its flexible and open development, is perfectly consonant with the activity of the Spirit 'really on the inside.' . . . The precarious fertility of cosmic history is not just the outcome of a drive towards complexity, but on its inside is the passion and action of the personal Spirit."

A Last Gasper

I had included this essay in several rewrites of the Guide but had concluded at one point that it should be left out. Mostly because it appeared to be "of interest only to the scientific mind and didn't have much to do with our actual recovery. " Then, one of my sponsees, who has a very high pressured career and was at that time involved with its most stressful activities; and also was experiencing several health issues that added to his stress. At that time it seemed important to me to send him this "essay" in an effort to convince him that working the Steps again would be very important at this time of his life and career. After he read it and contemplated on its deeper meaning he once again started through the Steps and to a commitment of daily meditation. Then he suggested that I include it in the Guide in a place where doubters and scoffers would probably never find it.

Earlier in the Guide I told the story of seeing Mt. Fuji from the deck of my ship when we were returning from Korea and had anchored in Tokyo Harbor for a short stop before heading back to the States. From where we were anchored I could see Mt. Fuji rising out of the surrounding Quanta Plains on an especially clear and beautiful sunlit day. Near the top of Mt. Fuji the blue sky blended with the mountain top and its snowcapped peak seemed to be setting on thin air above the mountain. I looked at that for a short while and then went back to work and didn't think about it for years.

During my early years of sobriety I was at an AA meeting at 26th and Broadway in Santa Monica, California, and a guy named Al S., with nearly ten more years' sobriety than me was sharing on meditation. He was talking about meditation helping us find out who we really are. He said, "Just as an experiment, close your eyes and see if you can visualize some memorable natural scene you may have witnessed sometime in your life. Some site such as Pike's Peak in Colorado, or Mt. Fuji near Tokyo, Japan." (I had to strain to not squeal Me! Me! Me!). Although I had not thought about that sight for some time I was able to picture Mt. Fuji in my mind's eye much like I had seen it years earlier. "If you can picture your scene in your mind's eye, see it and know that that scene is in your brain; and that who you are is the consciousness that is seeing the scene. Your consciousness is of your brain but is not your brain. You are the observer." That experience was an important motivation for me to commit to meditating every morning for at least thirty minutes for nearly 28 years without missing a day.

This essay is basically taken from a book titled *"Evolve Your Brain,"* written by Dr. Joe Dispenza and from its Foreword which was written by Dr. Amit Goswami. Drs. Dispenza and Goswami were both involved in making the Movie *"What The Bleep Do We Know?"*

Dr. Goswami briefly introduced some interesting features of Quantum physics, including the fact that it contains fundamental problems of interpretation. Quantum physics does not reveal objects as determined things but as 'waves of possibilities.' In fact, the brain is made up of quantum possibilities before we consciously observe it. Your consciousness is the primary material of your reality. Your conscious observation consists of choosing from the possibility wave the one characteristic that becomes the actuality of your experience. Physicists call this process the collapse of the quantum possibility wave. Where and how we place our consciousness, what we place our consciousness on, and for how long defines us on a neurological basis.

Dr. Dispenza explains that by placing our attention on fear we actually make fear exist because circuits in the brain that perceive fear become electrically activated by our attention. If we put our complete attention on something other than fear, the fear circuits shut off and the fear goes away. By controlling our internal circuits, independent of external environment, we can change our experiences. We choose to remain in the same circumstances because we are addicted to the emotional state they produce and the chemicals that awaken that state of being. We choose to live stuck in an attitude because a portion of the brain has become hardwired through repeated thought and reactions, and that limits our vision of what is possible.

I believe the following quotation from Dr. Albert Einstein is closely related to the forgoing explanation of the relationship between the brain and consciousness, although Dr. Einstein argued throughout his scientific career that "God does not play dice with the Universe." Nevertheless, in a letter to a man whose son had died from polio Dr. Einstein writes, "A human being is part of the whole called by us 'the universe,' a part limited in time and space. He experiences himself, his thoughts and feelings, as something separated from the rest---a kind of optical illusion of his consciousness. The striving to free one-self from this delusion is the one issue of true religion. Not to nourish the delusion but to try to overcome it is the way to reach the attainable measure of peace of mind."

Working the Steps in sequence as a way of life, changes our brain circuits from self-centeredness to God Centeredness with the corresponding collapsing of possibility waves onto more pleasurable experiences.

Guided Meditation on the First Three Steps

§

WHEN I WAS WORKING MY way through the Steps again in 1985, I started a Meditation process on the first three Steps while I was working on my Fourth Step. Frank had taught me to think of meditation as being conscious of what I want to be conscious of. That how I saw myself after meditating on what I wanted to meditate on as self-examination. That prayer was consciously aligning myself with what spiritual ideas I was being conscious of. Now please join me in being conscious of how the Big Book describes the alcoholic and alcoholism in part one of the first step; how it describes our 'lack of power' in Part Two of the first step; and, how the 12 and 12 describes our personal powerlessness in part 3 of the first step. Then following the guided meditation through Steps Two and Three were helpful to me in experiencing a new level of personal powerlessness that I think is required for each succeeding Step.

Be conscious of the language that describes the First Step: "We admitted that we were powerless over alcohol—that our lives had become unmanageable." Now, read the step over again being aware of the deeper meaning of each word and phrase. Then, once again, be conscious of the language describing Step

One, part one: 'We admitted we were powerless over alcohol.' Being conscious of the meaning of those words and phrases, continue along with the description of the alcoholic and alcoholism: "Alcoholics are men and women who have lost the ability to control their drinking." The loss of control is characterized by the insane obsession each time they start to drink that somehow, someway, this time they will control and enjoy their drinking. This time it is going to be different. Now the Big Book also tells us that coupled with that insane obsession is a physical reaction to alcohol that is peculiar to alcoholics as a class of people, which manifests itself in the phenomenon of craving for more once they start to drink. That this craving is stronger than their will power not to drink and the craving forces them to continue to drink. Alcoholics "... are restless, irritable and discontented, unless they can again experience the sense of ease and comfort which comes at once by taking a few drinks"---drinks which their insane obsession convinces them they can take with impunity. "After they have succumbed to the desire again, as so many do, and the phenomenon of craving develops, they pass through the well know stages of a spree, emerging remorseful, with a firm resolution not to drink again. This is repeated over and over ..." and over any considerable period of time it always gets worse, never better, "which leads in time to pitiful and incomprehensible demoralization." Now, if you are conscious of the deeper meaning of these descriptions of an alcoholic and alcoholism; and if you see that these descriptions fit your experience with drinking alcohol very closely, you now fully concede to your inner most self that you are an alcoholic. Be conscious of that truth for a few moments. Now fully concede to your inner most self that if you drink again you will almost immediately return to pitiful and incomprehensible demoralization. Also concede that in and of yourself you cannot stop drinking, you need help to do that.

Step One, part two: We admitted, ". . . that our lives had become unmanageable." Being conscious of the deeper meaning of each of those words and phrases, we continue with the meditation in the second part of the First Step. The Big Book tells us that when we 'Fully conceding to our inner most self that we were alcoholic" that is the first step in recovery. But then it tells us that alcohol is but a symptom of a deeper problem. That an alcoholic ". . . is like an actor who wants to run the whole show; is forever trying to arrange the lights, the ballet, the scenery and the rest of the players in his own way. If his arrangements would only stay put, if only people would do as he wished, the show would be great. Everybody, including himself, would be pleased. Life would be wonderful. . . . What usually happens? The show doesn't come off very well. He begins to think life doesn't treat him right. He decides to exert himself more. . . . Still the play does not suit him. . . . He becomes angry, indignant, self-pitying. What is his basic trouble? . . . Is he not a victim of the delusion that he can wrest satisfaction and happiness out of the world if he only manages well? . . . Selfishness---self-centeredness! That, we think, is the root of our troubles." If you have been conscious of this description of alcoholic behavior, and if you see that your behavior fits this description like a robin in a nest, then you can now, quietly, fully concede to your inner-most self that you lack the power to control your life so that you can experience happiness and satisfaction. Sit quietly and be conscious of the truth that essentially the only problem you have experienced is that you were not having your way; and that lack of power is your dilemma.

Step One, part three: "Our admissions of personal powerlessness finally turn out to be firm bedrock upon which you may build happy and purposeful lives." Now be conscious of the truth that whatever power you do have you did not give to yourself; all of our power comes to us from some other source of power. This has been true at the foundation of creation and is still true as "creation' continues to unfold.

We can stand on that knowledge as firm bedrock and build happy purposeful lives by now looking at Step Two: "Came to believe that a Power greater than ourselves could restore us to sanity." The Big Book tells us "that as soon as we were able to lay aside prejudice and express even a willingness to believe in a Power greater than ourselves, we commenced to get results, even though it was impossible for any of us to fully define or comprehend that Power, which is God." . . . "As soon as we admitted the possible existence of a Creative Intelligence, A Spirit of the Universe underlying the totality of things, we began to be possessed of a new sense of power and direction. " . . . "The prosaic steel girder is a mass of electrons whirling around each other at incredible speed. These tiny bodies are governed by precise laws, and these laws hold true throughout the material world. Science tells us so. We have no reason to doubt it."

Again, following Step 11 in the 12 and 12, "meditation, self-examination and prayer, logically interrelated and interwoven, form an unshakeable foundation for life." Close your eyes and focus your attention on your breath coming in and going out. As you bring the fifth in-breath in be conscious of the fact that your lungs filter oxygen out of the incoming breath and channel it into your blood stream where molecules of oxygen bond with molecules of iron in your hemoglobin. This weak bond holds the hemoglobin together while it is pumped to tiny capillary veins. There the oxygen and iron de-bond and the oxygen is transformed into carbon dioxide and nutrients are released from the hemoglobin and pass through the walls of the capillary veins to give new life to all of the cells in your body. You then exhale carbon dioxide into the air. Plants absorb the air and circulate carbon dioxide through their systems to give their cells new life, and convert carbon dioxide back into to oxygen and release that into the air for our next breathing cycle. Shift your consciousness back to your breath and with the next in-breath repeat the mantra "The Spirit of God is within me," and be conscious of that as truth; then on the out-breath repeat the mantra "The Spirit of God surrounds me." Repeat that for five breaths.

NOTE: If I was going to meet the President of the United States in the Oval Office I would probably be alert and excited with that experience. When I am consciously meeting God face to face I should likewise be alert to what I am really experiencing. Be awake to that Presence and Power!!

On the sixth out-breath shift your attention to your weight on your seat. That is gravity holding your body securely to the massive body of earth. Every massive body is made up of tiny particles whirling around each other at incredible speeds and in accordance with precise laws. These laws hold true throughout the universe. Science tells us that there are four forces of nature embedded in these particles, and that three of these forces are trillions of times stronger than gravity but all of the particles are so perfectly distributed and the forces of nature are so perfectly balance, that they are neutralized and gravity becomes the dominant force of attraction between all massive bodies in the Universe, holding it together as a single significant whole. Be conscious of that truth and then, as you breathe in know 'the Spirit of God is within me, 'and breathing out: 'the Spirit of God surrounds me.' Be conscious of the actual Presence of the Spirit of God underlying the totality of things for the next six in and out breaths.

On your sixth outgoing breath, shift your consciousness to your mind's eye. Imagine you are looking up at the stars on a very dark, very clear, moonless night. From that spot you can see hundreds of thousands of starts that appear to be closer than you have seen them before. Yet science tells us that the closest star to the earth is over 4 light years away and that the most distant star is a little less than 100,000 light years away. Your vision is principally interactive with the laws of physics governing light transmitted from every star. The same is true for light from Andromeda, our nearest galaxy being 2 million light years away. The fact that our recently created visual systems are principally interactive with light generated and transmitted from stars before you existed presents strong evidence of the pervasive presence and power underlying the totality of things. As you breathe in know 'the Spirit of God is within me;' as you breath out, 'the Spirit of God surrounds me' for the next five breaths.

Now, lets' go back to the Big Book statement, "Science tells us so. We have no reason to doubt it." Now Bill gives us a basis for a giant leap of faith: ". . . the perfectly logical assumption is that underneath the material world and life as we see it," (not just the physics and chemistry of life but the circumstances and events of life; the character and quality of those circumstances and events) "there is an All Powerful, Guiding, Creative Intelligence. . . ."

Being convinced, we were at Step Three and we thoughtfully pray the Third Step Prayer: *"God,"* stop now and be conscious that we are addressing "the Spirit of the Universe, underlying the totality of thing," . . . having "All Powerful, Guiding, Creative Intelligence," manifesting "precise law" order and harmony . . . and we pray: *"I offer myself to Thee---to build with me and to do with me as Thou wilt."* Stop now and be conscious of the truth that everything in life I need to fulfill my purpose will be drawn into my life and I have been given the power and knowledge to interact with those circumstance and events, practicing patience, kindness, tolerance and love, and to feel the unfolding goodness of my life. This consciousness will, *"Relieve me of the bondage of self, that I may better do Thy will."* Now stop and know that the underlying Spirit does not experience difficulties, problems or unresolved circumstances; those are the product of my thinking, actions and efforts to control things that I lack the power to control. Know that the Spirit only knows unfolding order, harmony and goodness. Knowing that truth will: *"Take away my difficulties, that victory over them may bear witness to those I would help of Thy Power,"* (which is all the power that there is in the Universe ;) *"Thy*

Love," (Love in which the Spirit experiences in every aspect of all being, and if I love my life I will be face to face with the Spirit's love of my life)*"and Thy Way of life"* (knowing that God's way of life is to grace His creation and His creatures with His Spirit for their goodness, then my way of life should be to be of service to God's creation and creatures for their goodness) *"May I do Thy will always."* Here we can pause in silence and be conscious of God's pervasive presence. When this presence begins to diminish in your consciousness you can bring it back by repeating the mantra: "The power of God is within me. The Grace of God surrounds me." In this way we can extend this conscious contact with God for a longer period of time.

Taking the first three steps as they are outlined here every morning while we are working the Fourth Step will build neuro-pathways that enable us to be conscious of God's presence. An important by-product of this practice will be to help establish a more personal relationship with the Spirit of the Universe that will be helpful in working the Fourth and later steps.

Also, stopping, as you go through the day, when you become agitated or doubtful, to become conscious of the pervasive presence of Divine Order in your life and to repeat the third step prayer will keep you in closer contact with your Higher Power. This will have the effect of shutting down your fight or flight center and activating your pleasure centers. I am not sug-gesting that you are going to have a "breath of Spirit from the mountain top going through and through," but that gradually, you will discover a sense of ongoing well-being, a sense of ease and comfort, which you probably cannot find in any other way. "This is a fact for us." I want you all to join me in doing this daily, and throughout the day, whether you are a newcomer or an old-timer.

Next, be conscious of Dr. Einstein's description of what he termed a Cosmic Religious Experience, where: "…the individual feels the nothingness of human desires and aims; (Step One) and feels the sublimity and marvelous order that reveal themselves both in nature and the world of thought. (Step Two) He looks on his individual existence as sort of a prison, and longs to experience the Universe as a single significant whole." (Step Three) Be conscious of that description of a spiritual experience and be conscious of how well it fits your experience in taking the first three steps.

I offer this Guided Meditation through the First Three Steps, for you to actually follow; or, to use as a guide to develop your own meditation. But I encourage doing this meditation practice. My experience has been that I went deeper into all three steps through this repetition; and I strengthened my consciousness of the presence of the Spirit of the Universe in my life during the meditation and throughout my day.

"We alcoholics are undisciplined. So we let God discipline us in the simple way we have just described." (Big Book, page 88)

BIBLIOGRAPHY

Anonymous Authors' "Pass It On: Bill Wilson and the A.A. Message," AA world Services, 1984

C., Chuck, "A New Pair of Glasses," New-Look Publishing Company, 1984

Cady, H. Emilie, "Lesson in Truth," United School of Christianity, 1955

Eddy, Mary Baker, "Science and Health with Keys to the Scriptures," First Church of Christ, Scientists, Boston, Mass., 1875

Dass, Ram, "A Journey of Awakening: A Meditator's Guidebook." Amazon Kindle, 1990

Dispenza, Joe, M.D., "Evolve Your Brain." Amazon Kindle, 2007

Doidge, Norman, M.D., "The Brain That Changes Itself," Penguin Books, 2007

Drummond, Henry, "The Greatest Thing in the World," World Bible Publishers, 1894

DuPont, Robert L., M.D., "The Selfish Brain," Hazelden, Century City, Minnesota, 2000

Ferris, Timothy, "The Whole Shebang," Simon & Shuster, N.Y, N.Y, 1997

Fitzpatrick, Mike, "Dr. Bob and Bill W. Speak," Hazelden, 2012

Feynman, Richard et al, "The Feynman Lectures on Physics," Addison-Wesely, 1977

Fox, Emmet, "The Sermon On The Mount," Harper-Collins, 1938

Gitlow, Stanley, M.D., "A Pharmacological Approach to Alcoholism," Grapevine, October 1968

Holmes, Ernest, "The Science of Mind," Penguin, 2010

Huxley, Aldous, "The Perennial Philosophy," Harper and Brothers, 1945

Miller, Kenneth R., PhD, "Finding Darwin's God," Harper Perennial, 2007

Newberg, M.D., D'Aquili, Eugene, M.D., "Why God Won't Go Away," Ballantine Book, 2001

Polkinghorne, John, "The Faith of a Physicist," Fortress Press, Minneapolis, 1996

Rohr, Richard, "Falling Upwards," Patheos, 2011

Rohr, Richard, "Immortal Diamond," Amazon Kindle, 2013

Taylor, Jill Bolte, PhD, "My Stroke of Insight: A Brain Scientists Personal Journey," Amazon Kindle, 2009

Teresi, L., M.D. and others, "Hijacking The Brain," AuthorHouse, 2011

The Layman with a Notebook, "What Is The Oxford Group?" Oxford University Press, 1936

The Dalai Lama, "An Open Heart," Time Warner Trade Publishing, 2006

W., Bill, "Alcoholics Anonymous, Second Edition" Alcoholics Anonymous World Services, 1955

W., Bill, "Alcoholics Anonymous Comes of Age: A brief History of A.A." A.A. World Services, 1957

W. Bill, "Twelve Steps and Twelve Traditions," AA World Services, 1952

Made in the USA
Columbia, SC
03 April 2019